Home Remedies

Also by Christopher Fahy

The Compost Heap (a novel)

HOME REMEDIES

*Fixing Up Houses and Apartments,
Mostly Old but Also Otherwise*

Christopher Fahy

Illustrations by Phyllis Cross

CHARLES SCRIBNER'S SONS, NEW YORK

In this book the author recommends certain products and services on the basis of his personal knowledge, and he also recommends sources that he considers reliable. But, of course, he cannot guarantee the quality, price specification, or safety of any of these products or services. So you should thoroughly investigate before buying or using any of them.

Before construction or even planning, please check with your local building and zoning codes to be sure that your ideas are within the limits set by local ordinances.

Library of Congress Cataloging in Publication Data

Fahy, Christopher.
  Home remedies.

  Bibliography: p. 219
  Includes index.
  1. Dwellings—Maintenance and repair— Amateurs' manuals.
  2. Dwellings—Remodeling—Amateurs' manuals.
I. Title.
TH4817.3.F33   643'.7   74-32200
ISBN 0-684-14220-1

3 5 7 9 11 13 15 17 19 C/ C 20 18 16 14 12 10 8 6 4 2

Printed in the United States of America

To my father, William Fahy, my father-in-law, Herman Sernoff, and Dick Orff of Philadelphia, Pa., and N. Waldoboro, Maine, who put up with me.

And to 334 N. Lawrence Street and 117 N. Lambert Street, Philadelphia, and Wallston Road, Maine, three implacable instructors.

My thanks to the National Gypsum Company and Owens-Corning Fiberglas for answering some tricky questions.

Contents

PUTTING THINGS BACK TOGETHER

Introduction:
My Old Places

I'LL NEVER DO IT AGAIN

When Davenc and I got married we moved into a one-bedroom box with a kitchen the size of a closet, a bathroom the size of a safe, and a closet the size of a cake of soap. The apartment was half an hour from downtown Philadelphia by public transportation, and it was cheap and warm. However, being ungrateful, unsatisfied types, we longed for more. Much more. We longed for space, for privacy, for a center-city location, *and* at the same or a slightly higher price than we were paying for our out-of-the center cell. We got it.

We got it because we were willing to fix up a crumbling, worn-out, leaky but large flat on the edge of a redevelopment area. The landlord supplied us with all the plaster, paint, and other materials, and promised us that if we did a decent job he'd keep the rent low for as long as we lived there. We got a bathroom (chilly), a gigantic kitchen, a living room, and three nice-sized bedrooms for only five dollars a month more than we had been paying for our box. Actually the place was not a total wreck: the previous tenant, with the same fix-it-up arrangement as ours, had done a year's sporadic plastering, painting, and patching before committing suicide. (No kidding, he really did commit suicide. Whether there was any connection between the work and his death, we never learned.)

It took us about two months of spare time to make the place livable. (We lived in it while we were fixing it, "livable" or not.) We didn't do a perfect job, just stuck everything together and made it look nice, but it was enough to satisfy both ourselves and the landlord. We did some foolish, tiring things that weren't necessary, but by and large we had a lot of fun.

We lived there a year and a half before the Philadelphia Redevelopment Authority took the building and forced us to move. Our successful fix-up experience encouraged us to try to find a wreck of a house, cheap and close to center city, that we could renovate ourselves.

We found one. The windows at 334 N. Lawrence Street were broken and boarded up, the outside trim had forgotten what paint felt like, the cellar was full of trash. One of the chimneys had fallen down. The bathroom was a second-story shed doing its best to say good-bye to the rest of the building. Its toilet and sink were smashed. The kitchen ceiling had decided things were safer on the floor.

But to our naive and optimistic eyes, the rest of the place didn't look too bad. It had good-sized rooms, most of the walls and ceilings seemed sound, the inside trim was pristine compared to our apartment. There was a beautiful stairway with a graceful bannister, four bedrooms, an attic with two more rooms, and the cellar full of trash was huge and not terribly wet. The roof seemed in good shape. The heater was a wreck, but the water pipes and radiators seemed okay. And the house was solid. *Solid.* You could jump around to your heart's content and nary a tremble. They wanted $4,000 for it. We needed a place to live. We bought it.

I can say now that it was one of the best moves we've ever

made. We wound up with a beautiful house, lots of room, and no mortgage. Our taxes, utilities, and maintenance over the six years we lived there averaged $50 a month. It cost us $8,000 to fix the place, but this was money saved, not spent. The house acted as a forced savings plan, and when it came time to buy our next wreck, at Lambert Street, we had enough for a good down payment and a lot of the renovations. We never would've saved that money otherwise.

But at the time, it was not so easy to see what a good deal we had. After our first month of work on the place we felt like kicking over our propane torch and collecting the fire insurance. We had made a big discovery: *It is impossible to tell what an old place is going to need until you get under its skin.* Just about every time you tear something out, you'll find some unexpected treat like a sawed-off rafter, or broken studs, or totally decayed plaster, or a rotted sill. Even the obvious things take far more time to fix than you'd ever guess at first glance.

So, here is point one. Whenever you consider fixing an old place, sit down and figure out how much time each part of the house will require, add it all up, then double it. Chances are it will take even more time than that. If it takes less, you'll be ecstatic. But if you don't follow this advice, brother, will you ever be depressed.

On Lawrence Street, we had the plumbing, heating, chimney, and electrical work done for us, as well as some of the major carpentry. Still, what we did—minor carpentry, cementing, tearing out, scraping, burning, plastering, painting, refinishing floors—took two years of our time. Well, not quite, because there was a period of about four months or so when I could not seem to get my brain to give the proper renovation signals to my arms, hands, eyes, and legs. Everyone I know who has tackled a major renovation has suffered from this strange disease.

So maybe twenty months of more or less steady work, and we were done. Some help from our friends, but not a whole lot. Now twenty months doesn't seem like a terribly long time, but at the end of it, no, months before the end of it, I said to myself, to Davene, and to anyone else who came by, "I'll never do it again." Everyone I know who has undertaken a major renovation has also, at least on one occasion, said the same thing. You say it when it appears there is no end in sight to the work, the dust, the clutter and the smell, no end in sight to the cracks, the holes, the leaks. Unfortunately this "no end" feeling continues until you are just about finished. Then suddenly the whole thing comes together and it's over. And after about a year of doing almost nothing on the place, your heart does not stick in your throat when you think of starting all over again somewhere else.

Which is what you may have to do if the highway comes through your house and you don't have a whole lot of money. Which is what happened to us on Lawrence Street. Actually we did have four years to live there after our work was finished, so things weren't as bad as they might have been. But giving the place up sure wasn't easy. Fixing a house is an intimate proposition. You get to know its every inch, and when you leave it, it's like leaving a friend. (If you have the kind of job where you're likely to be transferred every three years, I wouldn't advise renovating an old house. I wouldn't advise it—but maybe you'll like the work well enough and can detach yourself from the house enough to do it.)

We came across 117 N. Lambert Street by accident. We saw a small ad for a house in the newspaper, went to look at the place from the outside, and weren't impressed. But the big old wreck with the "Sale" sign on it across the street caught our eye. We called the realtor and arranged to go through it.

No wonder it hadn't been sold in the year it had been on the market. It was three floors, two apartments. The first floor hadn't been occupied in ages; there was a quarter inch of dust on the bathroom fixtures. The owner had started some sort of renovation of the second and third floors years before, but had never finished it. One second floor room was sealed off from the rest of the house and reached by an unfinished stairway. Wiring hung out of the ceiling, the plaster was crumbling, and the walls were black with soot. The concrete in the basement had been chopped to pieces and lay there in large, ragged chunks through which a rusty brook meandered. The roof leaked. The heater was shot. The place had been broken up so badly with closets and stairways and unfinished powder rooms that the only thing that could have felt at home there was a minotaur.

We went through the place with another prospective buyer who just kept shaking her head. When we left, I started to shake my head too. "Not again," I said. "We just can't take on another job like this again. I have other things to do with my life than fix up old houses."

In bed that night I couldn't sleep. The solid timbers and high ceilings and the French doors leading to a little courtyard wouldn't let me sleep. At last I said, "Davene, I hate to tell you this, but I think we're going to buy that house." She was awake. "I know we are," she said.

So we went through the whole process all over again. This time it wasn't so bad, because we'd had some experience and knew not only what *to* do but what *not* to do. It took us (and our faithful electrician, carpenter, and plumber—the same crew we'd used on Lawrence Street) only four months to get the place into move-in shape. Of course, there was plenty to do after that, but we approached the work in a relaxed way, and by and large it went well. Especially since we knew that once it was done it was done, and we'd live in that place for the rest of our lives.

Three years later we decided to move to Maine. It wasn't really as sudden as all that; we had been thinking about it even before we bought Lambert Street. But that hadn't been the time to do it and this was.

So we took the money we got for our Lambert Street house and went to Maine and bought a huge, completely fixed-up Victorian mansion with all new wiring and plumbing and heating and . . .

Of course not. We bought a small, ancient, sagging frame

house that had been empty for years and was in as sad shape as either of our other two places. Maybe sadder. When I took a friend to see it before we started work on it he said, "Fahy, I saw your other places before you fixed them and they were bad, but if you pull this one off it'll be a miracle."

So we're doing it again. It is by far our most ambitious project. We've ripped out the walls, stuffed them with insulation and covered them again, torn up floors and put them down again, done the electrical wiring by ourselves, torn out a chimney, rebuilt the stairs, eliminated old doors and windows and cut new ones through. This time we did the work with two little boys pounding through the plaster dust. There is still more stuff to do on the basement, the roof, the outside walls, the inside walls, the floors; I don't think it'll ever end.

Why are we doing it still one more time? Well, for a lot of reasons, but probably most of all because once you start fixing up old places you're hooked, it gets in your blood. So now you've been warned: watch out for the disease. I've had a bad case, but now this is it, the end, I'm cured, once this is over I'm finished, I'll never, *never* do it again.

WHY BOTHER?

Why bother fixing an old house? Lots of people say it isn't worth it. By the time you get through putting all the needed time and money into the place, they say, you might as well have bought something new. Sometimes this is true and sometimes it isn't. It is likely to be true if you have the repairs done for you. As a matter of fact, an old place can easily cost *more* than a new one if you don't do a lot of the work yourself.

On the other hand, there are many old houses in this country that you couldn't duplicate today at any price. We just don't build houses now that have 2 x 12 joists that are really 2 x 12, or have five fireplaces (as Lawrence Street did), or that have curved doors that fit into curved walls, and mahogany bannisters and closets that are mitered and pegged—unless we are literally millionaries. And even if we are millionaires, we won't get what these old houses have because most of today's builders have never learned to do things these old ways. But even if you could find the craftsmen who had the skills, the finished product still wouldn't look the same. There is a mellow quality about old places that you just can't duplicate. And consider this, too: whenever you salvage an old house, you salvage an awful lot of wood, brick, metal, glass, and concrete that would otherwise go to waste.

An old wreck *can* give you a lot of house for a modest amount of money. This country abounds in vacant, rundown houses. Wrecks scare most buyers off; they look like total chaos, and people don't know where to begin on them. They are hard to sell and can be bought for very little. In the city of Philadelphia alone, there are thirty thousand of them. A lot of them are in areas you might not care to live in, but others are in fine locations. So pick out one that's in a good spot, is solid, requires no major structural changes, has plaster and woodwork in good condition and details such as mantels, fireplaces, and bannisters intact. (Lots of luck.) And make sure you get it cheap. ("Cheap" is of course a relative term and depends on the prices of other houses in the area.)

Even if you have the wiring, plumbing, heating and other major jobs done by others, if you will do the minor carpentry, repair the walls, ceilings, floors, windows, doors, do all your own painting and some other miscellaneous repairs, you will save a

of money ove   d place.

renovate in your spare time, not during working hours. And secondly, believe it or not, chances are you will do as good or even a better job than the professionals. The reason? It's your place you're working on, and you care about it. Unfortunately, most of today's contractors only care about getting paid, and paid plenty.

Consider these gems: An electrician installs a switch box and accidentally saws a stud in half. (This can be serious—we'll go into studs later.) Another one hooks up his wires so that when you turn on your hair dryer, the lamp across the room lights up. Here's a favorite: the plumber hooks the hot water pipe to the cold water faucets.

Aside from these mistakes (all taken from real life) there are the deliberate, premeditated crimes: In order to run his pipes as quickly as possible, a plumber bashes a couple of studs out of his way and leaves them hanging. The carpenter covers the rotten window sills with aluminum and the soggy plaster with new plasterboard, but does nothing to cure the reasons for the rot. He removes a support in the cellar crawl space, forgets about it, remembers on the day the job is supposed to be finished, and replaces the post with a pile of loose stones. I've seen all this and much, much more.

I have also seen the incredibly shoddy work in new construction. A couple of years ago I looked at a ninety thousand dollar sample house in Philadelphia's Society Hill out of curiosity. The baseboards didn't match, the plasterboard seams were lumpy, the heating ducts were stuck in ragged holes. The bannisters were 2 x 3s nailed to wood cleats attached to the wall. One good yank and I could've had them off.

When you do the work yourself, you not only try to do the best job you home repair has sprung another problem—the problem of getting someone to do small jobs. If you have a minor roof leak, a crack in your plaster wall, or a broken window, you better know how to fix it yourself because your chances of getting a repairman to fix it are very slim indeed. If you want someone to put on a whole new roof or replaster your entire house, you'll have better luck, but no one wants to handle the little stuff.

My father's neighbor recently had a small leak in his roof. He saw an ad in the phone book, "Roof repairs—no job too large or too small." It was a local company and he thought he'd give it some business. The man came out in a huge car, looked around, sucked on his cigar, and said, "Pal, it just don't pay us to do a job like this. Now if you want us to coat the whole roof . . ."

My father didn't even come that close with his roof problem. He was pretty sure where the leak was and he figured he could fix it himself if he could reach the spot, but he didn't want to climb around up there. So he called half a dozen roofers for an estimate but none of them was interested. He didn't know what to do. Then he saw an ad for a huge long caulking gun. He bought it, put in a cartridge of roof cement, and was able to reach the spot and patch the leak himself. It cost him over thirty dollars for the gun and cement, which seems like a lot, but no one would've done the job for less than twice that price, if they ever would've done it at all. And my father has the gun in case another problem comes up. The sad fact is that unless you have a few hundred bucks worth of work for the man, he doesn't want to see you.

You're not convinced yet? Think about the skyrocketing cost of labor.

Several years ago (in Lambert Street) we wanted to cover a hallway ceiling with plasterboard. I would've done the job myself, but I was short on time. Davene said we ought to get an estimate.

"The materials will cost us twenty dollars," I objected, "but those guys will want ten times that much."

"That's impossible," Davene said. "It'll cost a hundred dollars at the most."

The man came over, pleasant, portly, prosperous-looking. "You did okay on the walls," he said a bit sheepishly, "why don't you do the ceiling?" "Time," I explained. He did about fifteen minutes of calculation, then looked up, smiled, shook his head and looked down at his pad again. "I got a crew, a secretary, a wife, and three kids," he said, "and we all like to eat." I had a vision of an office jammed with men, women, and children in coveralls, up to their jaws in roast beef, mashed potatoes and peas. "What's the estimate?" I asked. The man shrugged pleasantly. "Four hundred and twenty dollars."

So we scrounged huge cardboard boxes from a furniture store, cut the sides out of them, glued styrofoam cups to the cardboard and stapled the panels to the ceiling with our staple gun. The whole project was done in the evenings, after work. Total cost: Fifteen dollars.

THE TWO BEST REASONS

Fixing an old place makes you a more competent person. It gives you more control over your life. The more you do, the more you are willing to tackle. And when a crack appears or a window falls out, you don't panic and pick up the phone and pick up the phone and pick up the phone and beg, you fix the thing. It's a good feeling to have that confidence and that independence.

And finally, when you do the work yourself, the house becomes truly yours. You'll enjoy living in it far more than you would if you had it all done by somebody else.

So it pays to fix old places. But only if you like that kind of work, aren't afraid to get dirty (and cut sometimes) and above all only if you have patience. If you don't have patience, forget it and take up law or surgery.

One suggestion: before you become involved with an old house, get some experience. Fix an old apartment first, or help some friends with their wreck. This taste may convince you that you really have no interest in fixing up old places, or that you could never go through the ordeal that your friends are going through. It's nice to know these things before you have a deed in your hand.

WHAT THIS BOOK IS ABOUT

When I started fixing old houses I read every home repair book in the library, good or bad, and once you take the plunge, you should do the same. Before you start any job that's new to you, read as much as you can about it, decide which version makes the most sense (the home repair field is riddled with contradiction and confusion), plan how you're going to go about things, and assemble the tools you'll need. You may decide that some of the methods I propose sound crazy. If so, try another way. Experiment. You may find a new and better path.

This book is a history of my trial and error. It is not a comprehensive guide to all aspects of remodeling. Instead, it's the story of what I've come across and how I've dealt with it. If you do over an old place you'll run into a lot of the same kinds of problems I've run into, and this record of my experience should be helpful. Here are the jobs that this book will discuss:

• Demolition work. Just by doing all the tearing out yourself, you can save a lot of money. And if you do it yourself, you won't run into the horror of coming home and finding that your carpenter has torn out the closet in the bedroom instead of the one in the bathroom.

• Repairs to walls and ceilings. Even major repairs are within the scope of the amateur. You can fix small cracks and large breaks, cure flaking and peeling, fix holes in plasterboard. You can build partitions and closets.

• Floor repairs, from fixing loose boards to sanding and refinishing the living room and laying a resilient tile floor in the bathroom.

• Repairs to doors and windows. Fixing your old window sash and getting them to work right, replacing glass, putting in new sash, hanging doors.

• Caulking, insulating, and weatherstripping, to make the house weathertight.

• All interior and some exterior painting.

• Minor roof repairs.

The codes may stop you from doing much electrical or plumbing work, and you'll probably want a pro to handle such things as a new heating system or chimney flue. But we'll talk about this too.

If you aren't prepared to do this much, you will probably not save money by buying an old house, though you may still have some fun and end up with a terrific home. Of course, there's lots more you can do, but these are the things you should expect to do, and the things this book is about.

A word of caution: Don't do too much of any one thing at once, or you'll get sick of it. You'll get sick of the whole thing somewhere along the line anyway, so there's no use rushing it. After months of hard labor you'll look around at your seemingly pitiful progress one beautiful beckoning weekend morning and conclude that you simply cannot work on the place that day; or the day after, either, or the day or the week after that. Some people say to resist this urge, to fight it and carry on, or you will never get done. I say don't fight it. There are times when you have had it, both physically and psychologically. Take a break. Do something completely different. When you return, you will work with more spirit and things won't look so hopeless. A month away ought to do it. More than that, and maybe you *won't* ever get back into it again.

TAKING THE PLUNGE

1 GETTING INVOLVED

IT LOOKS WORSE THAN IT IS AND IT'S WORSE THAN IT LOOKS

What can be wrong with old houses? Just about anything, and any old place that's been sitting vacant for a while is bound to have plenty of problems. Your major concern, though, is with the building's structure. No matter how hopeless and desolate an old place looks, if its structure is sound, it can be made into a comfortable and attractive place in which to live.

One point: defects are easier to spot in old run-down places than in old fixed-up places. You can cover up all kinds of big troubles with a piece of plasterboard, and people do it all the time. I'd rather buy a wreck than a place that someone's fixed up. You can stab and bang and scrape at a wreck with impunity and find out a lot of its terrible secrets before you put your money down.

3

Basic Structure

Stand close to the walls of the house and look up toward the roof. Do the walls seem to bulge? Are there any cracks in them? Look especially closely at the corners of the house. I have seen several city houses where the walls have parted company at the corners. Tying them together again is a job for a pro, and it's expensive.

Does your city row house have metal stars or squares on its front? These are braces put in at one time to keep the walls from buckling. Don't mess with houses like these unless there's really nothing else around. Braces don't mean that the place is about to fall down, but they do mean that there's a potentially big problem.

Check the cellar joists and the roof rafters for rot. Stab any suspicious-looking spots with an ice pick to see if they're soft. Check the joists most carefully where they come into contact with masonry. Check rafters closely around chimneys; this is where roof leaks frequently occur. Old frame houses rest on large timbers that sit on top of a stone foundation. These timbers are called sills. Stab these with the ice pick every couple of feet. See if there are long rounded lines of mud about ½" or so wide on the joists and sills. These "mud tubes" were built by termites. The devils may have left for greener pastures or may

still be there, but it will take an expert to tell. Does the floor dip
or bounce? Are there posts supporting the joists in the cellar?
Are there stains on the walls or ceilings, suggesting a leaky roof ?
Does the roof sag? Does its surface look chewed up? Is the
chimney falling down? Is the basement floor damp? A damp
floor in the summer may be a frog pond in the spring.

If a house has a major fault in any of these areas you'll have to
think very carefully about buying it. Not that major faults can't
be repaired—they can be, but they are jobs for professionals,
and they will cost. The floors in my parents' house had to be
replaced completely, joists and all, they were in such bad shape.
That was over thirty years ago. Today such a job would be
prohibitive in cost to people who are looking for inexpensive
shelter.

An encouraging note: Most old houses, especially city row
houses, are structurally sound. A city block is more or less a
unit: the houses support each other. Or as someone said to me as
he showed me an old place Davene and I were thinking of
buying, "I won't guarantee the walls in the front and the back,
but it won't fall over sideways."

I have been in hundreds of old places, and only about a dozen
had severe structural faults. A lot of them had minor faults: a
few rotted joists, some sag, a crack in an exterior wall, a bulging
section of foundation. You can usually fix these things yourself.
If your house has rotten sills, though, it means jacking the whole
place up and putting in new ones. If your front wall bulges
badly, it will have to be rebuilt. This can cost you several
thousand dollars. You have to really be in love to mess with
things like this.

Mechanics

After structure, the mechanics of the house come next in
importance. This means the plumbing (including water heater),
heating system, electrical wiring, and chimneys. Take it for

granted that they are in bad shape and will need replacing, though maybe not right away. We have lived with a coal furnace converted to oil, falling chimneys and 60 ampere wooden conduit wiring while we were trying to scrape enough together to buy replacements. But eventually we did get replacements for the sake of efficiency, economy, convenience, and safety.

It is possible, of course, that even though the place is old, at one time or another an improvement was made that is still perfectly fine. Maybe someone had the place rewired, threw in some insulation or installed copper water pipes. Don't count on it. We have needed new heat, new electric wiring, and some new plumbing in all of our houses, and just about every old house we have looked at has needed them too.

Structural Alterations

You should also consider whether the basic arrangement of the house satisfies you. Major structural changes are very expensive. These include such things as moving a stairway or tearing out a bearing wall—that is, a wall that helps hold up the house. Don't plan anything like this unless it's absolutely essential. Try to arrange your living space so that the basic structure of the house can stay the same. (The basic structure does not include non-bearing walls—walls that simply partition off space. These can be torn out whenever you like. We'll discuss how in the chapter on walls.) Moving the bathroom, for instance, almost certainly means moving the waste line ("soil stack"), so see if you can keep it where it is. These structural considerations impose restrictions on what you can do with the place, but in most cases you will still have a lot of latitude.

The Rest of the Place

Aside from the stuff already mentioned, there is the condition of the interior walls and woodwork, the doors, the windows, the floors, etc. There will probably be something wrong with all of these. Sometimes they look just terrible, but a little scraping, filling, and painting will bring them up fine. Other times they don't look bad at all. Then you take off a spot of ugly wallpaper—and the plaster behind it falls on the floor.

INSPECTION SERVICES

Okay, you're scared. You've had no experience inspecting old places before. You think you see something terribly wrong, but you can't be sure. You jump up and down on the third floor and it bounces and the windows rattle. This can mean loose windows and loose floorboards, or it can mean a calamity. How can you tell which?

Without experience, you can't. If you know an architect or contractor who knows what he's doing, have him check out the place with you. If you don't know anybody, the best thing to do is consult a home inspection service. Look up "Home Inspection" or "Building Inspection Service" in the yellow pages of the phone book. If there are no such listings, call a realtor who does appraisals, he may be able to provide the same service.

At present it costs $50–$100 to have a guy come out, go over the building thoroughly, and write up a description of everything he finds wrong. He won't tell you whether or not you should buy the place, that's up to you, but he'll tell you what you're in for. The service is well worth it as far as I'm concerned, though I've never used one because I've known people who would do the job for free.

Whatever you do, don't listen to the realtor who shows you the place. He is working for the seller, not for you. When you ask him if the roof leaks he will tell you, "I never saw it leak," even if half the ceiling has fallen away. When you mention the bulging front wall he will say, "The place has been standing for a hundred and fifty years and it'll stand another hundred and fifty years." Don't bother trying to prove to him the lack of logic in this statement.

We once pointed out some major faults in a house to a realtor right after he showed us through. He denied the faults and at last became so defensive that he finally insisted that all the place needed was a little paint. He ended up shouting, "Well if you think this place is so bad, why don't you buy that old wreck across the street?" As things turned out, that's exactly what we did.

WHAT IS THIS GOING TO COST?

The information you gather on your inspection (or through your inspection service's inspection) is essential to your estimate of what it'll cost to fix the place up—that is, the contractor costs and the costs of the work you will do. You usually have to figure all this out by yourself, even the contracting, because contractors generally will not give you estimates before you actually put money down on the house. How do you go about drawing up your estimate? One good source, if it is available to you, is friends who are renovating. They can give you some idea of what the various jobs will cost. Home magazines also sometimes have lists of average costs for improvements.

It's hard to give such figures in a book because they change so rapidly (always in an upward direction), but for those of you with no conception at all of the money involved, here's a rough idea of what you'll pay for major jobs:

A complete electrical rewiring, including a new 200 ampere service but exclusive of light fixtures, will cost about $1,500. (Fancy light fixtures can cost a bundle.) If you're just having a few new outlets put in, they'll run $10–$25 per box (including wiring).

New copper waste and water lines to one full bath and one half bath (sink and toilet, no tub) and a kitchen sink should run $700–$1,000. (This is probably already an underestimate—the price of copper rises almost hourly.) The cost of three white bathroom fixtures—sink, toilet, tub—plus installation will be $600–$1,000. (Color costs more.) A new soil stack (the main waste line) can be a few hundred dollars if it's plastic, or over $1,000 if you're forced to use cast iron. A septic system is around $1,000, a well and pump $1,500 and up. A whole new kitchen with new sink, cabinets, counters, and all appliances can sock you $5,000 or more. (If you want to handle some of this yourself, you can cut down on this figure drastically, as we'll see later.)

A furnace alone should cost $600–$1,000 installed. A whole new warm air heating system including new ductwork will run $1,500–$2,000. A complete hot water heating system will cost more, about $2,000–$3,000. A new chimney two stories high is $300–$400. Asphalt shingle roofing costs $40–$60 per 100 square feet installed, but if the old roof covering has to be removed, it costs $85 to do the same area.

Depending on where you live, how big your house is, and your contractor, you may have to pay more than these figures or you may get away with less. In the city a carpenter may charge $10 or more per hour, in the country, $5 or less.

Next, check prices locally on lumber, plasterboard, paint, and other materials to estimate what your do-it-yourself jobs will run. Add everything up and stick on another 20 percent to play safe. It always costs more than you think it will. Is the purchase price low enough to justify this outlay? One thing for sure: unless you get the place dirt cheap, it is not worth buying if it needs a major structural repair such as a new front wall.

If you're only looking for an apartment, breathe a sigh of relief, you don't have to bother with all this stuff. You just want to make sure the place isn't going to fall over, you can stay reasonably warm in it, and the plumbing and electricity function.

2 DEALING WITH CONTRACTORS

YOU CAN USUALLY GET THE KEY TO AN OLD WRECK AS SOON AS you put down your "earnest money." This is the deposit you give to the realtor when you sign the agreement of sale—usually 10 percent of the purchase price. You can also usually get permission to start knocking things apart before you actually take title. On Lambert Street I put in a full month of demolition and repair before the place was really ours. Watch out though! Don't sink your time and energy into a house unless you're sure it *will* be yours (as I did in Maine—and then almost didn't get the place).

As soon as you have access to the property, line up some contractors for estimates. This way they'll be all set to start as soon as you become the owner.

You may want to have a general contractor handle all the work you won't be doing yourself. This will cost you more than if you hire a separate plumber, electrician, etc., because you're paying the general contractor to supervise these subcontractors. Another minus in this arrangement—you have to use the men he chooses, and someone may have told you of a great electrician

10

or a super plumber whose rates are super too. But you can't use them if you have one man direct the whole operation. I prefer to deal with separate contractors, one for each major area. But there are minuses here too: it means more personalities to deal with, more people to keep bugging, and you may not feel up to it.

HOMEWORK

Before you have anyone look at the place, go to the library and read up on the jobs you want done. See how the descriptions in the books relate to the problems you're facing. When the contractor comes, you'll know some of the terms he uses, know what questions to ask, and not look completely foolish.

You don't want to antagonize professionals by pretending to know more about the work than they do. But if you read up in advance, you'll pretty much know what's involved in a job. The more recent books will also tell you about new developments in the professional's field, and it's important to know about these. It's surprising how often a contractor has never heard of the things you will read about in books. He usually learns how to do a job a certain way, with certain materials, and it takes an awful lot of persuasion to get him to try something different. If the guy strongly resists changing his way of doing things, don't fight it, unless his way seems completely wrong to you. Doing things differently takes time, and in the building trades, believe me, time is money.

On the other hand, contractors will often use methods you never read about in books. These are things they've learned through trial and error or have seen work for others. These things they trust. Ideas taken out of some book by a guy who sits in an office all week, they do not trust.

Some of the tricks these guys come up with are tremendous

work, time, and money savers. Other things they come up with are not so tremendous—like using caulk in twelve-degree weather when the cartridge says to apply it only when the temperature's above freezing. They will cling tenaciously to notions that are flatly contradicted by everything you read in books or on the packages of materials. To get them to do things the way you want them done, you'll have to be a diplomat.

FINDING A CONTRACTOR

Where do you find a good contractor? Friends and neighbors are the best source. When you're at someone's house and see a piece of work you like, find out who did it. The work speaks for itself and you pretty much know what you'll be getting. Of course if the friend says the cost was three times what someone else paid for the same job, you may have second thoughts. Get acquainted with some people in your new neighborhood. There is almost always someone around who can give you a couple of names. If you have a mortgage, the bank that holds it may suggest someone to you. You may know an architect who is familiar with contractors in your area. Or you may arrange to have a part of the work done, some carpentry let's say, and when you see what a fine job the guy does (usually it is a guy), you can ask him if he knows a good plumber or electrician. This procedure is a little risky, because the guy is apt to pick a friend rather than the best mechanic, who may be his mortal enemy.

SCARE TACTICS

The home remodeling field has its share of bad guys, so be on the lookout. I've run into several of them. One kind tries to scare you so much you'll be willing to pay him anything if only he'll remove the source of the threat to you and your loved ones. I once had some men come out to give me an estimate on lining a chimney. The chimney I wanted repaired was not in use, and there was a hole in it where a heater stovepipe used to vent. One of the men ran his hand solemnly around the hole until it was good and black, and held it up to the other man. "Look at this, Ed," he said. The other man examined the hand and shook his head. "Wow," he said. "What is it?" I asked, my heart in fourth gear and dollar signs blurring my eyes. "You're living on a bomb," the first man said, "this stuff is like gunpowder." Ed nodded. "The heat from a forty watt bulb could blow this place sky high." My heart quieted down. "No kidding," I said, showing them the door. "I'll have to remember to use only twenty-five watt bulbs in that chimney." Fortunately I had done my reading beforehand and knew this was one of the biggest rackets around.

SHOPPING

Get three estimates on any job you want done. Why three estimates instead of two, or thirty-eight? Because three is a magic number. Actually, I don't know why. Get as many estimates as you need to feel comfortable, but get several, the price range can be startling.

By the time we bought Lambert Street, we had lost track of Dick, our Lawrence Street carpenter. Rumor had it that he'd moved to Maine. A friend told us about a guy who did all the carpentry work for one of the local colleges. He came out reeking of booze one sunny Saturday morning and suggested all sorts of outlandish solutions to our problems. His estimate was $2,000. Unimpressed, we called someone else. We wanted to have some steps extended as part of the job. "Well, we'll take the horse and put it . . ." The guy looked puzzled. "No, we'll put the horse . . . Wait a second, if we put it . . ." This did not inspire us with confidence. Two weeks later we hadn't received the estimate, so we called the outfit up. We didn't want them to do the work, but we wanted the estimate. They had no record of coming to see us, so they sent another guy who looked the house over quickly and asked us how much it had cost. I told him and he sniffed, "And that's how much you'll sink into the place before you're through." His estimate for the carpentry work: $2,200.

A cook at the school where Davene worked had a husband who was a contractor. He was thoughtful, level-headed, and had some good ideas. We were pleased as punch. The estimate? $3,200.

A week or so later the telephone rang through our gloom. "Hi, this is Dick, I hear you've been looking for me." As usual, his ideas made more sense than anyone else's, and his estimate was $1,800.

FREE ESTIMATES

Watch out for contractors who won't give free estimates. There may be some reputable people who operate this way, but I wouldn't count on it.

When we bought Lambert Street, I got the name of a heating contractor from a friend who'd just had central air conditioning installed. I called the contractor up, he said he'd be glad to give me an estimate, but it would cost twenty dollars. He'd refund this money if I decided to have him do the job. If it hadn't been for my friend, I would've dropped the thing right there, but I was anxious to have the work done, had inspected my friend's air conditioning and found it fine, and so foolishly I said okay.

The guy came over, measured the place and said he would get

back to me. I paid him the twenty dollars. Three weeks went by, no estimate came, and I couldn't get an answer when I called his number. My job sent me out of the state for the summer. All through July and August I waited for an estimate in the mail, but got none. When I returned to Philadelphia in September, I called the guy for two weeks without success. Once I got his wife, who said he'd call me back, but he never did. Finally I got him at eight o'clock on a Monday morning. He was probably waiting for another call and I'd caught him by surprise. He vaguely remembered me and was sorry he'd forgotten about the estimate. He was also sorry that he couldn't do the job because one of his men had quit and he was short-handed. What about the twenty dollars I had paid him? He was sorry about that too, click.

I got the Better Business Bureau after him and the money came back in a flash. Be warned.

I'LL BE THERE FIRST THING
IN THE MORNING

Contractors never show up when they say they're going to. They will promise, absolutely promise you they will be there Tuesday at the latest. Then Tuesday comes and you chew your nails all day as the cellar fills with water. Contractors must take a course in this tactic; those who are punctual by nature are forced to change their ways. There's a logic to this: their erratic appearance helps keep you off balance, and while it may anger you, it makes you oh-so-grateful when they do appear.

Still, all this may enable you to get a clue to a guy's reliability right away: if he comes for the estimate on time, it's a hopeful sign. Or, to put things less positively, if he doesn't even show up on time for the *estimate,* you're in for it.

DEPARTMENT STORES

After our forty watt bulb fiasco on Lawrence Street, we heard of a masonry contractor who did great chimney work. We called Bonjourno and asked him to come out. "Sorry," the man said, "we're booked solid for at least the next six months, we can't even give you an estimate."

We didn't know where to turn. Davene saw a home remodeling ad from one of the local department stores in the newspaper. She suggested we give it a try. At least we would get the job done, and a big store would be more open to redress of grievances than a small contractor in case the work proved unsatisfactory. "They'll charge a fortune," I moaned. But I had no better suggestion and so I went along.

The store sent a man out, a rather confused little guy who couldn't seem to grasp what we wanted. I had done my reading, and I drew him a diagram of how I thought the flues might run. He looked at it, wandered around, mumbled a few things, and gave us an estimate. It seemed a little high but in the ball park, and we accepted it. He said he'd be back in a few days with the contractor and discuss the job with him.

About two weeks later he returned with the contractor—you guessed it—Bonjourno. He showed him my diagram, showed him the chimney, and kept saying, "Cement around, you know?" while moving his hand in a circle. Lou Bonjourno nodded, looked up the flues with a mirror and said nothing.

When the job was halfway finished, Lou came around to inspect the job. He took me aside. "Tell you the truth," he said, "I don't know how —— can do this for the price they quoted you. If you'da dealt directly with us, we'da charged you at least two hundred dollars more."

So using a department store doesn't always mean the job will cost you more money, or that the work will be inferior to that of an independent contractor. It may mean you'll get the job done faster than you would otherwise.

But remember that the contractor's allegiance in this case is to the department store, not to you, and you will probably find that your discussions with the workers will have a rather remote quality.

Here's another plus for department store mechanics: they will have workmen's compensation, so in case they break a leg in your bathroom you won't get sued; and liability insurance, so that if they wreck your dining room more than they fix it, they will pay to undo the damage. We have friends whose electricians kicked a hole in their kitchen ceiling. The insurance paid for a complete repair. Liability insurance and workmen's compensation are two good things for any contractor you employ to have.

CONTRACTS

You should sign a contract with your mechanics, or you're likely to find the cost of the job go up and up as the work progresses. Some guys will tell you it'll cost you less if you don't sign a contract with a fixed price, but don't worry, it won't.

SPECIALISTS

Here's something you may not expect: Electricians, plumbers, and some other specialists will do work only in their areas and in no other. This means that if you have the outside alley drain dug up and replaced, the plumber will put the dirt back in the hole, but he won't cement over it. The electrician will chop holes in your walls to run lines and install boxes, but he won't plaster them up again, you'll have to hire a plasterer or do the job yourself. (Electricians *will* nail down any boards they pry up, however; I guess they're afraid you'll break your neck and sue them.)

When you get your estimates, be sure to find out what work is not included in the job. This will save you disappointment and some angry words. One advantage of having a general contractor supervise the whole deal is that all these little details are taken care of.

LEARNING FROM YOUR CONTRACTORS

You want to be around some of the time when your contractors are working. You don't want to bug them to death, but you do want them to know you're concerned. And you also want to learn as many of their tricks as you can. Watching a guy install a window or plaster up a hole can make things an awful lot clearer when you try to do the same jobs on your own. These guys have learned by doing, and no matter how much you read, you're going to learn the same way.

No matter how good or honest or pleasant contractors are, I'm always glad when they're finished. There are days when they don't show up (for no apparent reason) and you wonder if they ever will again. Then when they do show up they make so much noise you can't think. If you have old materials around that you want to save, they'll use them one day while you're gone. "Oh you wanted that wood in the corner? That old piece of pipe?" And you'd better hide your tools or they're likely to use them, too.

When the job is done, check it carefully. If there's anything you're unhappy about, have it corrected before you make the final payment, or believe me, you'll never see the guy again, I don't care if he's your uncle.

3 TOOLS AND MATERIALS

POWER TOOLS

MUCH OF THE WORK ON OLD HOUSES CAN BE DONE WITH HAND tools, but there are a few power tools that will make the work go much easier and are well worth the investment.

An electric drill is just about indispensable. You will use it thousands of times, not only for making holes, but also for sanding, buffing, removing screws, etc. The most practical drill for the kinds of work described in this book is the ⅜" variable speed, reversible drill. (The ⅜" refers to the widest size drill bit shank that will fit into the chuck—the part of the drill that opens and closes to hold the bit.) The variable speed feature is great: you start to bore a hole in metal or other hard surfaces very slowly, then increase your speed (by pulling the trigger back farther), and your bit doesn't skip around all over the place. As soon as you buy your drill, attach the chuck key (the thing you

19

tighten the chuck with) to the power cord with a piece of string, or you'll lose it.

Get a set of bits for your drill. One standard kit has thirteen bits that range in size from $\frac{1}{16}''$ to $\frac{1}{4}''$ in width. Be sure to get good bits: cheap ones will go through wood, but give you trouble on metal. The handy-person will rarely have to drill a hole wider than $\frac{1}{4}''$ in metal, but if he does, larger bits are available. You will likely have cause to drill holes wider than $\frac{1}{4}''$ in wood—when installing latches, locks, running electric wire through studs, etc. Wood boring bits—for use on wood only—generally range from $\frac{3}{8}''$ to $1''$ in width. For drilling even wider holes in wood, you can buy a hole saw with various sizes of interchangeable blades. This attachment fits right into your drill like an ordinary bit. Masonry bits will cut into brick and concrete. And if you plan to use a lot of screws in your projects, it might pay you to purchase screw bits. They drill and countersink a hole that's exactly right for the screw you're using. You can buy them for any size wood screw.

The second most valuable power tool to have is a circular saw. I use a $7''$ (this refers to blade diameter), but you may find that too heavy and want one smaller. A "combination blade" will both crosscut (cut across the grain) and rip (cut with the grain) and also cut fine enough for most of the carpentry jobs you'll run into. A tungsten carbide-tipped blade costs twice as much or more than a regular blade, but it stays sharp much longer.

I don't have the space to explain how to use these tools, you'll have to go somewhere else for that. But just let me warn you that a circular saw is a powerful tool and must be handled very carefully. When using it, don't support the part of the board you're cutting off, or the saw blade will bind and kick back at you. After the first time this happens, you will develop a remarkable respect for your saw. Or maybe even a fear of it. Always move the blade through the work slowly, never force it, and be careful when you set the saw aside: the still-spinning blade can do a lot of damage. Some saws have brakes that stop the blade the instant you take your finger off the trigger, a tremendous feature, but quite expensive.

Another handy but not indispensable power tool is the saber saw. It lets you cut curves in wood and is great for cutting sink holes in countertops, notches in studs, etc. Get one with a trigger control so you can stop it immediately if there's any trouble.

Get a 50-foot, #16 or #14 wire extension cord to use with these tools. Most power tools are now double insulated and no longer have the 3-prong grounding plug. If you have the 3-prong plugs, naturally you'll need a 3-prong extension.

HAND TOOLS

The first hand tool you should buy is a medium-priced screwdriver. Beat the devil out of it, then use it ever after for prying up lids of paint cans, removing moldings, scraping, gouging, and stabbing. Then you'll never have to wreck any of your good screwdrivers doing these things.

Get a set of four good standard screwdrivers and a couple of Phillips screwdrivers. You'll rarely find a Phillips screw in an old place, but the new hinges and locks and other hardware you buy will frequently have them. Of course you'll need a claw hammer, a plane, a pair of pliers, and a crosscut saw. Buy a vise for your workbench. You should have a hammer with a 40 ounce head for bashing things. You will need a 3″ putty knife, a 1¼″ putty knife, a small pointing trowel, and a rectangular plasterer's trowel. A wire brush is useful for all sorts of cleaning jobs. You will need a caulking gun.

A level is essential. They come in all different lengths; 2 feet is a good size for the handy-person. A staple gun is a tool that will save you loads of time and trouble. Be sure to get a heavy duty one.

Some good saws to have on hand: a hacksaw (you'll probably

run into some pipes that you'll have to cut out of the way, and you're sure to come across some rusty bolts), a backsaw and miter box for cutting moldings, and a keyhole saw. Rub a little oil on your saw blades and they'll cut faster. I would also recommend a small bow saw, a tool usually used for pruning trees and cutting firewood. It is very good at cutting through old joists, studs, rafters, and windowsills. It is inexpensive and easy to handle. You can get one at Sears.

Buy a good-sized adjustable wrench, a pair of straight-cutting sheet metal shears, and some wire cutters. Get some needle-nose pliers for the tight spots. Arc joint pliers, pliers with very long handles, give you a lot of leverage and will loosen nuts that other pliers won't budge. This is a very useful tool.

You'll need a couple of sizes of wood chisels and several cold chisels for chopping into brick and concrete. You'll want a pry bar for tearing up floors and ripping out old lath and sheathing. A nail set looks sort of like a short, metal pencil. You use it to sink nails below the surface of a board. People often forget to buy this little tool. Get one, you'll need it. An awl or old ice pick is good for starting screw holes. Get a utility knife for cutting plasterboard and other such things. (They aren't expensive, so get the best you can buy.)

You will need a steel square, a yardstick, and a steel tape measure. The yellow tapes are easier to read than the white ones. And the kind where the tape sticks straight out rigidly and locks in place anywhere along its length is far superior to the standard kind—you don't need to hold the end of the tape while you measure. Stanley's "Powerlock" tapes are excellent. Buy a large rubber eraser for removing erroneous pencil marks on studs, etc. Get a couple of files and a sharpening stone. Dull tools are murder to work with.

A glue gun is nice to have around but not essential. A propane torch comes in handy on a lot of jobs; you'll probably find you'll need one sooner or later. And get a good pocket knife. A good knife is joy, a bad one misery.

You'll want gloves (I prefer leather), plastic goggles, and maybe a face mask for dusty work (face masks always suffocate me and I don't often use them). The jelly-type hand cleaners that come in a can will take grease and paint off your hands better than anything else, and with less irritation. You can clean paint brushes with them too.

Buy a solid, sturdy aluminum stepladder, one with at least a 250 pound rating. The extra money is worth it for the added security. You'll be up on the ladder plenty, and it's spooky to stand on something that shifts and shakes.

With these tools you'll be able to do just about anything to an old house. There are a couple of other special tools that you'll need for certain jobs, and I'll mention them when we get there.

Now this may seem like a lot of tools to buy. You may not need all of them, it depends on the kinds of jobs you have to do, and you don't have to buy them all at once. But if you do buy them all, they'll cost about $350, or just a little more than you'd pay a $6–per hour carpenter for seven days of labor.

RENTAL TOOLS

There may come a time when you'll want an electric cement mixer or a sanding machine or some other piece of seldom-used equipment. You can often rent such things from hardware stores and paint stores, and many cities have branches of national rental firms like American Rental Service and United Rent-All. Look under "Rental Service" in the yellow pages.

MATERIALS AND SOURCES OF SUPPLY

Your old wreck will hurl you headlong into a foreign and not always friendly world, the world of hardware and building supply. The guys in these places can tell instantly that you're an amateur, and they'll delight in subjecting you to a mild form of fraternity initiation. At first all is utter confusion, and they will do little to dispel it. If you keep cool and bear the humiliation nobly, you will be accepted into the charmed inner circle—at just about the time you're finishing your house.

Two little games in these establishments deserve special mention. Number one is the game of "Whatever you call it, I'll call it something else."

For example, you go into the building supply and ask, "You got any waterproof wallboard?" (*Never* say, "Do you *have* any waterproof wallboard?") The guy behind the counter frowns and says, "Green drywall?" You say, "Yeah, that's it."

Now if you had come in and asked, "You got any green drywall?" the guy would've frowned just as deeply and said, "Waterproof wallboard?" If you ask for "stool cap," he'll say, "Window stool?" If you say "blue nails," he'll say, "Sheetrock nails?" and vice versa. There is no way around this game except to say something like, "You got any green drywall, otherwise known as M-R board, waterproof or water-resistant wallboard, plasterboard, Sheetrock or tile base?" I wouldn't try it.

But even this method would do you no good, for the guy would simply shift right away to game number two, "Details." You spew out the above description and he says, "Half inch?" Then you have to admit that you don't know what thicknesses the stuff comes in. As far as I can figure, this is the point of the game. The guy will never say, "Yes, we have it in $\frac{3}{8}''$, $\frac{1}{2}''$, and $\frac{5}{8}''$, which thickness would be best for your purposes?" That would take all the fun out of it. The only solution to this one is to read up on all the characteristics of whatever it is that you're buying before you ever set foot in the store. But don't worry, you still won't win, they'll trip you up somewhere along the line.

Your primary dealings will be with a hardware store and a lumberyard or building supply house, which handles lumber and a lot of other building materials as well. If you live in a metropolitan area, you may also be able to deal with masonry, roofing, and electrical supply houses. In a less populated, area, the building supply will handle all of these materials. The hardware store is for locks, doorknobs, bolts, screws, etc. You can often buy plaster, cement, and roofing materials there, but you shouldn't, because they are going to cost you a lot more than they will elsewhere. If you want roofing materials, go to a roofing supply. I once saw a gallon of roof cement on sale for $1.95 in a hardware store, $1.35 in the building supply, and $.95 at the roofing supply. A bag of perlite plaster once cost me exactly twice as much at a hardware store as it did at a masonry supply house.

Shop around for your materials. One lumberyard may have plywood $4 cheaper than another one a few blocks away. Their 2 x 4s, on the other hand, may cost 15 cents more apiece. If you're buying in any quantity, this makes a big difference. If you're having stuff delivered, make sure to ask if there's a charge. If the answer is yes, it may wipe out your savings on materials.

A word to city dwellers about deliveries. More and more frequently, a place will only deliver to your door (or sidewalk, to put it more precisely). In Maine, the guys will take the stuff into your house and put it where you want it. In the city they are likely to put ten bags of concrete mix on your pavement and take off. Of course, if you start waving dollar bills around, they may reconsider.

Lumber varies markedly in quality. Try to find a place where they will let you pick it out yourself. The large, self-service types of operations are best for this. This way you can get 2 x 4s that are suitable to build with. If you have them delivered sight unseen, you may end up with a pile of hockey sticks.

For those of you unfamiliar with the world of wood, you have to know that lumber has nominal dimensions and actual dimensions. At one time 2 x 4 lumber was actually 2″ thick in one dimension and 4″ thick in the other. You will find studs like these when you tear old walls apart. (Studs are the vertical members of wall framing.) Nowadays a 2 x 4 is roughly 1½″ x 3½″ thick, and still shrinking. Likewise a so-called one inch board, ⅞″ thick not very long ago, is now ¾″ thick. A 1 x 5 board is actually ¾″ x 4½″. This follows the rule, "Anything newer is thinner." New moldings, hinges, new *anything* look positively anemic beside their counterparts of years ago.

For studs, joists, and other "dimension lumber" (see glossary) subtract ½″ from the nominal dimensions to find the actual dimensions. Remember that "one inch" boards are really ¾″ thick, and deduct ½″ from their nominal width to find their actual width. *Lengths* of lumber, however, are accurate. If you ask for an 8 foot 2 x 4, it will be 8 feet long. Plywood, plasterboard, and paneling are full dimension. A 4 x 8 foot piece of plywood is exactly 4 x 8 feet—unless they cut it wrong.

Don't buy better quality materials than you need, if you can help it. If you're going to cover a countertop with plastic, tile or linoleum, don't go out and buy top grade exterior plywood, use particle board, which is much less expensive and perfectly satisfactory. Use sheathing plywood instead of finished plywood if a smooth surface is not important. Don't use 2 x 4s where 2 x 3s will do—for example in building a closet or a non-load-bearing partition. (I have, however, seen times when 2 x 3s cost more than 2 x 4s, so you have to be careful.) Try not to buy longer lumber than you need: 2 x 4s come in 7 foot lengths (good for framing doorways), and in 8, 10, 12, 14 foot lengths and longer; 2 x 6 and larger lumber doesn't come shorter than 8 feet, but if you're on good terms with your lumberyard they'll cut shorter lengths for you. They also sometimes have short pieces of stuff lying around, so ask.

Each time you waste 10″ or so of a 2 x 4, you cringe at what it's costing you. But it's surprising how many of these odds and ends you will use (as spacers, cripples, etc. [see glossary]). And then when you think of how much a carpenter would charge for the job you're doing yourself, you perk up rather quickly.

You don't often see air-dried lumber nowadays, most of it is dried in a kiln. Either drying method means that when you get the wood it's done most of its shrinking and twisting. You can frequently buy "green" 2 x 4s, studs that haven't fully dried out. They are cheaper than the kiln dried, of course, but they're risky for the amateur to mess with. Friends of ours had a carpenter build their stall shower out of them, and when the heat went on for the winter, the whole thing buckled and half the tiles fell off. Kiln dried studs usually have "kiln dried" stamped right on them.

If you tear out an old partition, you'll have a bunch of full dimension, sturdy studs on hand. (They are splintery, so wear gloves when you handle them.) Very often these have become bent and twisted over the years as the house has eased into a more comfortable position. Don't try to reuse twisted studs like these, they'll give you one devil of a time. If they're straight, great. But double check for nails before you saw them, or there goes your blade. Old nails are sneaky. They turn up in impossible places. Your carbide-tipped blade can hold up longer than a regular blade under their assault, but it won't last forever. You can buy special blades that will cut through nails, and it's good to use one if you plan to saw a lot of old wood.

USED STUFF

There may come a time when you'll want some old planks or beams or floorboards or doors for one of your projects. The wrecking (or "salvage") company is the place to go. These outfits have an incredible assortment of stuff that they've saved from their demolition projects. If you need shutters or anything else to fit an existing space, be sure to take the measurements with you, and take your tape measure too.

Cities often have firms that specialize in used kitchen equipment. You have to check out a used electric range carefully, because a lot of things can be wrong with it. Be sure to plug it in and see how it works before you buy it. A gas range is a simpler machine. The one thing you have to check closely is the oven control—but you won't be able to until the gas is hooked up, which won't be at the store. Don't buy a used refrigerator unless you *know* it's good. The freezer often doesn't work, and if the insulation on the power cord is bad you can get a dangerous shock. You can frequently find a steel cabinet sink with good faucets and acceptable finish for very little. On Lawrence Street we bought a gas range for fifty dollars and a large cabinet sink for fifteen dollars (and we didn't even have to replace the faucet washers).

You can sometimes find used wall and base cabinets at these places, but good ones are not as common as good sinks. The wooden ones you assemble yourself are made of good materials and the drawers slide very nicely. Sears and Wards carry them. The directions are a little confusing, but not terribly so. You can buy a kitchen full of these cabinets for $300. Remember, you don't have to use formica (tricky to install and finish) on countertops: paint or stain covered with three coats of polyurethane varnish will hold up very well. (If you use this finish, you'll probably want to replace the thin particle board tops with ¾" plywood.) These kitchen cabinets are fine in a playroom or bathroom, too, but they're too high to fit under a desk.

Another interesting source of used materials is a restaurant supply. Table bases, chairs, chopping blocks, etc. can be picked up cheaply. And don't forget the "thrift stores." I've found the Catholic charities, St. Vincent De Paul's, etc., have the best stuff at the cheapest prices. These places often have sinks and ranges, as well as good quality but out-of-fashion furniture. (Old sideboards with the legs cut off and a new finish make great storage cabinets).

MAGAZINES

Tools and materials change constantly. Read the ads in *Popular Science*, *Popular Mechanics*, *The Family Handyman*, and other magazines to keep abreast of the latest developments.

4 GETTING UNDER WAY

YOU CAN'T WAIT TO GET STARTED. YOU ARE BURSTING WITH enthusiasm and energy. You are eager to transform your incredible wreck into a safe and comfortable dwelling. Also you're starting to panic.

Before you touch a thing, make sure you know what you're doing. Resist that powerful urge to plunge in and tear the place apart. What comes down quickly goes back up very slowly. It is best to tear out as little as possible. Each little bit you rip up is not just more work and more mess, but also the hiding place for another thorny problem you'll have to wrestle with.

ARCHITECTS

If you're going to gut the place completely, or if you simply have no idea of what should be torn out and what should remain or how your space should be arranged, get the advice of an architect. This person can save you a lot of costly mistakes.

DIRTY WORK

Okay, once you definitely know what has to go, get rid of it. Get it all out right at the start. Demolishing even one tiny closet makes a fantastic mess, with plaster dust everywhere, and you want all this over with before you move in if you can manage it. You also don't want the electrician to run his wires over or through things you had planned to remove, or the plumber to run his pipes across them, so get it out now.

Before you tear out any walls, though, be sure they aren't holding up the house. (See the section on removing partitions.) And be careful when you smash things up outside. In tearing down an attached shed, I once took a good chunk out of the stucco on my neighbor's wall.

In the city, the most convenient way to get rid of huge amounts of trash is to call up a rubbish removal outfit, have a bin parked on your sidewalk, and toss everything into it as you go along.

Rip out all the old telephone wire before your new phone is installed, or you're stuck with it. But once you've taken it off, if it's the older, thicker, plastic-covered wire, hang onto it—it is absolutely great for securing things to the roof rack of your car. You don't have to tie the wire, just twist it and it holds. (The newer stuff is too flimsy to work like this.)

If you're taking off moldings and baseboards, do it as carefully as possible; you may want to use them again somewhere. They are expensive and often can't be matched unless you have them made up special.

Sometimes you take off something you're going to put back in the same spot again. Write down how it came apart, draw a picture, number the pieces, and tie them together or put them in a box. "Oh, I'll remember how that goes," you say to yourself. Then you get sick or go on a trip and when you look at the pieces again they're a mystery. And mark them with dark *pencil.* Once I retiled a shower. As I took off each tile, I carefully numbered it with a felt-tipped pen. When I went to put the tiles back, the numbers had faded to little gray smears. Some fun.

Scrape and hammer crumbling plaster off the walls and ceilings. Scrape off the old wallpaper. (A real job; I'll discuss it later.) If you have calcimine on the walls, remove it (also discussed later). Sweep the dust off the ceilings, walls, and floor.

Then: Get some cheap white latex wall paint and paint the whole place, woodwork and all (unless the woodwork is natural or stained and you want to preserve it). Don't worry about the holes, go right over them. The paint will seal the remaining dust, make the place look cleaner, and generally stick things together. It will make you feel much better about the whole proposition. It will also brighten things up considerably. White reflects light better than any other color, and your light situation is not apt to be super for a while. You'll appreciate the paint's help. We didn't do things this way on Lawrence Street. After we tried it on Lambert Street we realized what fools we'd been.

The white paint will also help you to see minor holes and cracks. This way you won't spend your time patching defects that don't exist, or overlook cracks that blend into the mosaic of old glue, paint, and dirt. When the walls have been painted, go over the floors with a mop and wash the windows.

In this ripping out process you can find anything, so be prepared. Among other treasures, I've turned up a dead cat, thin and gray as waxed paper, pornographic books, an Indian-head penny, and a bottle containing a human heart. Yes, that's true. Who knows, you may be lucky too.

THE BASICS

Next, call in your plumber, heating contractor, and electrician. Before you do extensive work on the place yourself, you want these guys out of your hair. They may have to run a duct where you wanted a doorway, and you'd like to know this kind of thing as soon as you can.

Set up a workshop. Build yourself a workbench if you don't have one (*America's Handyman Book*, an excellent, comprehensive home repair manual, has a simple, functional plan), and stick up some shelves for your tools, paints, and other supplies. Most people, including myself, don't spend enough time on this step, but if you can get organized right from the start it will save you an awful lot of grief later on.

Decide on the order in which you will work on the rooms. You should get the kitchen and at least one bedroom in shape before you move in.

HOW GOOD A JOB DO YOU WANT TO DO?

There will be plenty to do, so concentrate on the essentials. Once they're done, you can spend all the time you want on elaboration. In an old apartment, you just want to stick the place together, get it reasonably clean, attractive, and comfortable. You don't want to put much money into it unless you know for sure that you can stay there for years. You may not want to sink a whole lot of money or labor into an old house, either. Consider each project carefully before you begin. Why people who buy old houses seem to be afflicted with grandiose ideas, I don't really know. The guy has a shack, an absolute wreck, and he says, "As soon as I get this place cleaned up, I'm going to build a hand cut, pegged spiral staircase." "I don't really like pine floors," says another guy surveying his decayed monstrosity, "I think I'll tear them up and put down walnut." I'm not making this up, I really heard people say these things. You think you're immune to this disease? So did I. I haven't done anything really crazy (I don't think), but I sure have entertained some pretty wild notions. All I can say is, watch out.

WHAT WILL THEY LET YOU DO YOURSELF?

Most communities have some kind of building code. Go to your city hall or town office and find out what the code covers before you start work.

The contractors you hire will know about the codes relating to their specialties and will take out any required permits (or at. least they should). In most places you are allowed to do pretty much anything in your own home except for plumbing and electrical work. But find out. The "urban homesteaders" in Philadelphia have to get not only the electric, plumbing, and heating done by professionals, but also the roofing.

PUTTING THINGS
BACK TOGETHER

5 YOUR WALLS

BUILDING A PARTITION

YOUR OLD PLACE WILL NEED PLENTY OF WORK ON ITS WALLS. Before you tear any out or fix any up, you ought to know how they're made. And the best way to learn how they're made is to build one. (Not that you'll actually build one before you patch some cracks or tear one out, but we'll pretend.)

Chances are you'll build a stud wall in your house somewhere along the line. You may want to divide a large room into two smaller rooms, or even tear out an entire floor and partition it off in a different way. Maybe, like Lambert Street, your third floor is one huge room and you don't want to leave it like that. Old places are notoriously short on storage space, and you are likely to build several closets. Building a closet is basically the same as building a whole wall, so let's discuss wall building.

A partition is a wall that serves primarily to divide space within a building. It consists of a frame (usually studs) and a

37

skin (most often plasterboard or plaster). We will build one for privacy. We want to cut out light and sound. We will not build our partition to hold the house up, and therefore it will not have to be built like an outside wall. Most partitions in old places are built like outside walls, though; that's just the way it was done—and often still is.

Here are the tools and materials you will need: Hammer, circular or crosscut saw, level, pencil and large eraser, steel tape measure, 10d (pronounced "10 penny"),* 8d and 6d nails, drill and bits, enough 2 x 3s for the job, and another person (optional but very helpful).

The biggest complaints against plasterboard partitions are their "flimsiness" and the fact that you can hear everything right through them. The second complaint is quite legitimate—you don't want to be bothered by noise from the room next to you. The "flimsiness" complaint seems mainly psychological—no less legitimate, but something you can learn to live with, and cut down on, if you build the wall a certain way.

One sheet of plasterboard will cut out light as well as two layers of lath and plaster can—or fifty feet of brick can, for that matter. It will not do much to cut out sound, and two sheets (one on each side of the wall) won't do much better. But it is possible to treat a plasterboard wall so that it has fairly good sound insulating properties, as we'll see later on.

You can build your partition out of 2 x 4s or 2 x 3s. The latter ($1\frac{1}{2}''$ x $2\frac{1}{2}''$, remember) are cheaper, lighter to handle, and will save you an inch of floor space over 2 x 4s. I'll use them in this example.

But: in some areas you may not be able to find 2 x 3s longer than 8 feet. If this is true where you live and the partition you plan to build is more than 8 feet long, it's better to use 2 x 4s,

---

* No one seems certain just how the term "penny" came to be associated with nail sizes, but the higher the number, the longer the nail.

which you can readily find 10 feet long and longer. Otherwise, you'll have to make the top plate (see below) out of two pieces of wood, and this isn't a good idea. And if your partition is higher than 8 feet and you can't get 8 foot long 2 x 3s, by all means use 2 x 4s—you don't want to piece studs together.

The partition framing consists of a 2 x 3 nailed into the floor (the "sole plate"), a 2 x 3 nailed into the ceiling (the "top plate"), and a number of long vertical 2 x 3s nailed between these two plates (the "studs"). To simplify things, let's have your partition run from one wall across to another wall—in other words, let's have it cut across a room. To complicate things, let's put a doorway in it.

You can't always put the partition just where you might want it (unless you go to some trouble), as we'll soon see. It depends on whether you're building it at right angles to the joists in the ceiling above it, or if you're building it parallel to these joists. But let's forget about this for the moment.

Take the straightest 2 x 3 you can find and place it on the floor exactly where the partition is to go. Mark along both sides of this 2 x 3 with a dark pencil, drawing its outline on the floorboards. You have just marked the location of your sole plate. Remove the straight 2 x 3 and put it aside. You'll be using it again.

If you have the door you're going to use, measure its width, add $\frac{1}{4}''$ (you need $\frac{1}{8}''$ clearance on both sides of the door), and mark this width on the sole plate outline at the spot where you want the door to go. Use a very sharp pencil. If you don't have the door, most come 24'', 30'', or 36'' wide, so take your pick and add $\frac{1}{4}''$. You can add a little *more* than $\frac{1}{4}''$ but *don't* add less.

On each side of this doorway opening, measure *back* $\frac{3}{4}''$ and draw a line. This is the spot where your door jamb will go. Now measure the thickness of your 2 x 3. (It's probably $1\frac{1}{2}''$, but it never hurts to make sure.) Mark this thickness on the outline right next to the $\frac{3}{4}''$ markings. This is the location of the short studs that hold the doorjamb. We'll call it the $1\frac{1}{2}''$ mark.

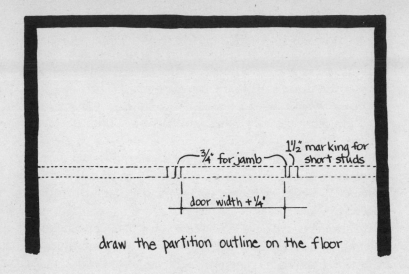

1½" marking for
short studs

¾" for jamb

door width + ¼"

draw the partition outline on the floor

Now lay a 2 x 3 flat on the floor beside the outline so that its end butts against a wall. Draw a pencil line on it at the 1½" mark you've made on the floor. Saw off the 2 x 3 just a tiny bit (about ¹⁄₁₆") short of this pencil mark. Then nail it into place on top of the outline. One end will butt against the wall, the other will fall just short of the 1½" mark. Don't let it extend over this mark, or your doorway will be too narrow. Cut another piece for the other side of the doorway and nail it down. Use 10d nails.

You will find that your nailing job will go much easier if you follow this tip: Pick out a drill bit slightly smaller than the diameter of the nail you are using and drill pilot holes through the 2 x 3 before you drive your nails. Don't drill into the floor, just through the 2 x 3.

A word about nails. A number of people have written about the inefficiency of the standard "bright common nail." Its holding power, they point out, is much less than a threaded nail, and significantly less than a galvanized nail, which has a rough or cement-coated surface. I always use galvanized nails because of their better holding power, but I don't use threaded (or

"ringed") nails. For one thing, they're hard to find—the closest
you usually come is underlayment nails. But even if I could find
them I wouldn't use them for partitions because I make too
many mistakes. Ringed nails are murder to pull out. I'd love to
tell you that I never nail a piece of framing in the wrong way,
but one lie would only lead to others. I find the combination of
the drilled hole and the galvanized nail the most practical for an
amateur like myself.

So you've nailed your sole plate in place. Now you have to
figure out where your top plate should go. Take your real
straight 2 x 3 again. Hold it upright this time, put one end on a
sole plate where it butts against the existing wall. Hold your
level up to the side of it and make sure the 2 x 3 is plumb.
("Plumb" means straight up and down.) Where the narrow sides
of the 2 x 3 meet the ceiling, mark the ceiling with your pencil.

Two people come in handy here—one to hold the stud and
use the level, and the other to do the marking. (You may have to
cut your 2 x 3 down some to get it to fit between the floor and
ceiling, but that's okay, you can use it as a stud later on.)

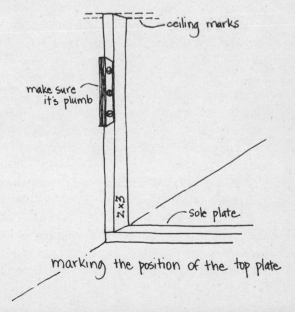

marking the position of the top plate

Follow the same procedure on the other side of the room. You have now marked the spot where your top plate will go.

Measure the distance across your ceiling from the one pair of markings to the other and cut a 2 x 3 to this length.

An important aside: This distance is likely to be either shorter or longer than the distance across the floor at the very same spot in the room. Never take anything for granted in old places. Memorize this axiom, "Nothing is level, nothing is plumb, nothing is square," and you'll be all right.

The 2 x 3 should be cut so that it fits snugly in its position on the ceiling. Stick it up there and nail it in place. This is hard for a person to do alone.

What do you nail the top plate into? If the partition runs at right angles to the joists (the beams that support the ceiling), you nail it into every joist it crosses. You have to find these joists by experiment, just as you'd find a stud . . . Tap on the plaster until you hit a spot that sounds very solid. Drill a tiny hole through the ceiling at this point. If you're lucky, you'll hit solid wood, a joist. You probably won't be lucky. Keep trying.

But if the partition runs in the same direction as the ceiling joists, you have to locate it directly under one of the existing joists to give yourself a nailing base. This is a pain, because it limits where you can place the partition. Joists are usually no closer than 16″ apart, and it's rare when you'll find one exactly where you want your wall to be. (It's even rarer to find one where you want your closet to be. You may be able to compromise on the location of your wall, but your closet may well turn out to be too shallow or too deep if you build it under an existing joist.)

If you've torn out your ceiling, there's no problem even if the partition runs parallel to the joints. You can nail pieces of 2 x 3 between the exposed joists. This "bridging" will give you a fine base for your top plate. Cover the bridging with plasterboard *before* you nail the top plate in place, and then you won't have to cut the plasterboard to fit around the plate later on.

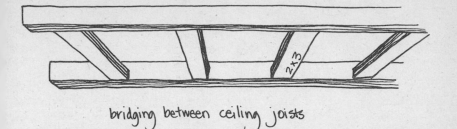

bridging between ceiling joists

Now you could use this same method with an existing ceiling
if you were willing to saw out the covering between one pair of
joists. If the material is plaster and lath, this is a real mess. If
your ceiling is plasterboard or insulation board ("celotex"), it's
not such a terrible job, and you might consider it.*

Let's say you've been lucky and you've got your top plate up.
Now you're ready to put in your studs.

The first studs you'll put in place are those that fit right next to
the walls. Since they butt against these walls, you won't have to
worry about them slipping out of place when you hammer them.
You will have to worry about slippage with your other studs, as
we'll see in a minute.

How can you measure the distance between the sole plate and
top plate accurately so that the stud will fit snugly? Take a scrap
piece of 2 x 3 and lay it flat on the floor beside the sole plate.
Hold a 2 x 3 upright and rest one end on this scrap, with its
inside edge touching the edge of the sole plate. Where the 2 x 3's
inside edge touches the top plate, make the mark for the cut.

Don't try to take this measurement by resting the 2 x 3 on the

---

* I've read that if your ceiling is *sound* lath and plaster, you can
anchor the plate in place with Molly bolts, but I've never done it.
In this case, you'd put the top plate in position, then drill through
it into and through the plaster and lath. Remove the plate and
insert the Mollies in the ceiling. Put the plate back up and screw
it into the Mollies.

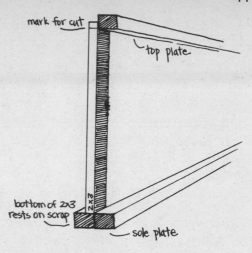

marking the length of the stud

sole plate itself; the stud will meet the top plate at an angle, and your mark will not be accurate.

Cut the stud about $\frac{1}{16}''$ longer than the spot where you've marked it. If you don't cut it longer, you'll probably find that your saw blade has taken off just enough to make the stud fit loosely, and you don't want that. You want to be able to tap the stud in place with your hammer so that it stands up without any nails. But you don't want it so long that you have to pound it into place; this will bow the stud, and you'll have a time trying to find it when you nail up your plasterboard.

Tap the 2 x 3 into place and check it with your level to make sure it's plumb on both its front and side. Next, toenail it into place. That is, nail at an angle through each end of the stud and into the plates. The first nail goes through the broad side of the stud and toward the wall. Use an 8d galvanized nail. Once the stud is secured in this fashion at both the top and bottom, drive 6d nails through its narrow sides and into the plates.

The stud is nailed in place against the wall. It is perfectly plumb. If it isn't, tap it plumb. You are going to want the rest of your studs to be either 16″ or 24″ on center from this stud—that is, you want a space of either 16″ or 24″ from the center of one stud to the center of the next stud. The 24″ spacing is okay, but it won't give you a solid-feeling wall if you're using 2 x 3s. It may make you feel more secure to have 16″ centers. It's up to you.

If you're using studs 1½″ thick and you set them 24″ on center, you'll have 22½″ between each stud. Cut a piece of scrap wood to this length (or 14½″ long if you want 16″ centers). This spacer board is more than a measuring device, it will also help you keep the stud in place while you nail it.

Lay the spacer on the sole plate, one end against the stud you've nailed in place. Its other end will give you the spot where you nail your next stud.

Cut a stud to the proper length, following the same procedure as the first time. (Don't try to cut all the studs at once to the same size as the first one. Unless you are very, very lucky, each stud is going to be just a little bit different in length because of irregularities in the floor and ceiling.) Tap the stud in place against the spacer board. Take a pencil and mark the sole plate where the stud meets it. Toenail your 8d galvanized nail about halfway in, then take out your spacer. If you don't get it out at this point, it'll get stuck and you'll have to pry it out. Once it's out, hammer your nail in the rest of the way. The pencil mark on the sole plate will let you know if your stud has slipped or not while you were nailing. If it has slipped, tap it plumb. (You don't want any studs out of plumb. You want to maintain that 16″ or 24″ on center spacing. Otherwise you'll have trouble putting up your plasterboard, and if you're going to insulate the wall, you'll have trouble putting your insulation in too.) After your first 8d nail is in firmly, put your 6d nails in the stud's narrow sides, then drive another 8d nail into the other broad side.

Put your spacer on the top plate, hold it in place with a nail driven in part way, mark the position of the stud on the plate, nail the stud into place.

Keep going like this until you reach your doorway.

An additional tip: If you have a lot of scrap wood around, you can cut spacers for between each stud and nail them permanently to the sole and top plates as you go along. This is very nice, because it makes it *impossible* for your studs to slip while you're nailing them. You don't need constantly to check them for plumb with your level, because you know they've stayed put. Even if you have to buy a couple of lengths of spruce strapping—cheap 1 x 3 furring strips—it may be worth the extra work and money to do it this way during your first shot at this kind of thing. Also: it helps to drill pilot holes for your nails. It isn't essential, but it helps.

Okay, you've reached the doorway. What now? All you do for the time being is nail a stud flush with the cut-off end of the sole plate. Make sure it's plumb. We'll call this the "doorway stud."

Now go across to the other wall and follow the same procedure all over again, building out toward the doorway. It is highly unlikely that the space between the "doorway stud" and the stud closest to it will turn out to be exactly 24″ or 16″ on center, but that doesn't matter.

When you have this much of the wall built, cut some 22½″ lengths of 2 x 3 and nail them horizontally between the (vertical) studs about 4 feet up from the floor. If you stagger them you won't have to toenail them, you can nail right into them through the studs. This bracing will give a firmer base for your plasterboard and eliminate some of the flimsiness I mentioned earlier. It will also strengthen your doorway. (If you're using 2 x 4s and ½″ plasterboard, this bracing isn't really necessary.) You can use one brace between each pair of studs for a wall up to 8 feet high, but use two between each stud for a wall higher than that. Your partition will now look like page 47.

Now it's time to make the door frame. If you have your door, measure its height. (The standard height is 6′-8″, but yours may be different.) If you plan to have a 1″-thick threshold, add 2″ to your door height and cut a 2 x 3 to this length. For example, if

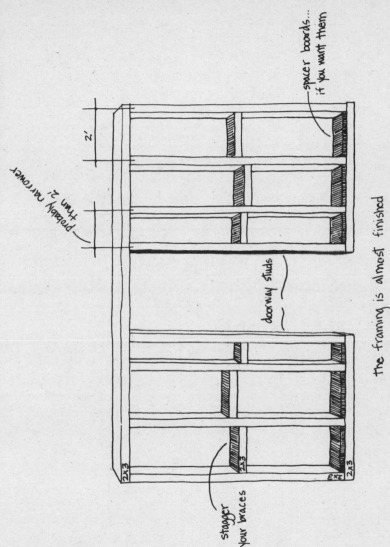

spacer boards...
if you want them

2'

probably narrower than 2'

doorway studs

the framing is almost finished

stagger your braces

2×3

2×3

you have a 6'-8" door and a 1" threshold, you'll cut your 2 x 3 6'-10" long. One extra inch allows for the threshold, the other allows for the top of the doorjamb, which will be installed later. We'll call this 2 x 3 we've just cut the "short stud."

Actually, with an inside partition, as we've been building here, unless you are covering some gap in the floor, or unless the floors on different sides of a doorway—the living room floor and the dining room floor, for example—are at different levels, I can't see much point to a threshold. It's just more work and something to trip over. If you decide to omit it, add only 1¼" to your door height to find the length of your short stud.

Now place your short stud up against one of the doorway studs, its bottom resting against the floor. Nail it into the floor, into the end of the sole plate, and into the doorway stud. If the floor slants a little across the doorway opening (that is, from left

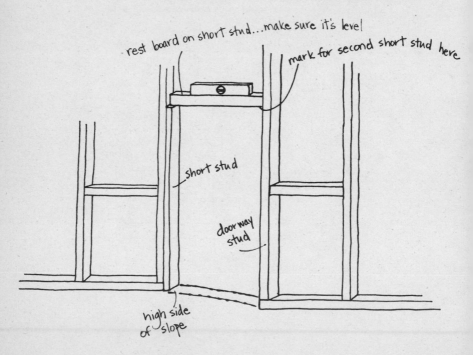

to right), nail this stud to the side of the opening where the floor is *higher.*

Now you have to cut a short stud for the other side of the doorway. If your floor is level, you can cut it exactly the same length as your other short stud. If your floor slants and you've nailed your first short stud to the high side of the slope, the second short stud will have to be *longer* than the first, or the doorway will be crooked at the top. If your floor does slope,

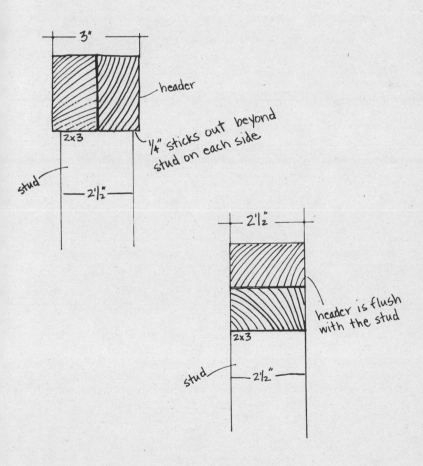

hold a board across the doorway from the top of the *short* stud you've already nailed in place to the opposite *doorway* stud. Make sure the board is level. Where its bottom meets the doorway stud, mark the doorway stud with a pencil. Next, hold a 2 x 3 up against this doorway stud, mark it at this point, and cut it. This is your second short stud. Nail it in place.

Next you want to nail a "header" across the tops of these two short studs. Cut two pieces of 2 x 3 so they just fit the distance between the *doorway* studs. Nail them together, making sure their ends are even. This gives you a header 3″ high and 2½″ wide. Set it across the doorway so its ends rest on the short studs. It should fit snugly.

Now the books always tell you to place these headers so that the 2½″ dimension faces the rooms and the 3″ dimension faces the floor and ceiling. The stiffness of the header is much greater when it's placed this way, but then you have a header 2½″ high and 3″ wide—and the short studs and doorway studs are only 2½″ wide. Now you obviously cannot have that extra ½″ sticking out from your partition, or you'll never get your plasterboard on right. It's a mystery to me how those books can tell you to set the header in this way and then not tell you how to resolve the problem of the extra half inch. So I don't put the header in their way. I haven't had any problems with sagging, but if I had a doorway wider than 30″, just to play safe I'd make the header out of *three* pieces of 2 x 3 instead of two. This should make it plenty stiff.* (See illustration p. 49.)

* If you're building with 2 x 4s, you'll find you have the opposite problem with your headers if you set them in the way the books tell you to. The 2 x 4s are no thicker than 2 x 3s. Nail two of them together and you still have a header 3″ thick. Install it the way the books tell you and you're now ½″ *short* of the surrounding studs. Here, though, you can get around the problem by putting a piece of ½″ filler in between the 2 x 4s before you nail them together, bringing the thickness of the header out to 3 ½″. You can use plywood, particle board, or even plasterboard, anything to keep the 2 x 4s spread half an inch apart.

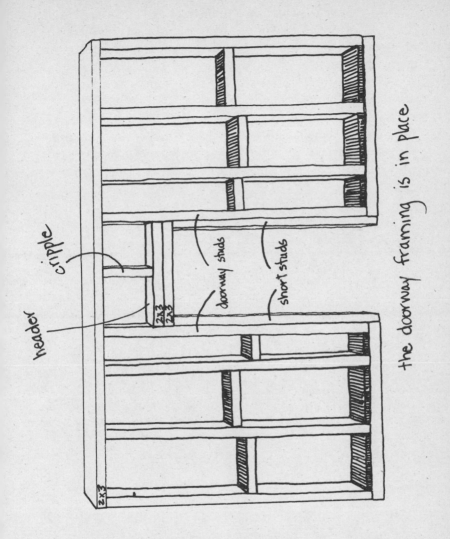

header
cripple
2x3
2x3
doorway studs
short studs
the doorway framing is in place
2 x 3

Once you've set the header in place, hold it there permanently by nailing into it through the doorway studs. Next, run a tiny stud up from the header to the top plate and nail it in place. This is called a "cripple."

Now your wall is completely framed in. We'll put the skin on later, in the section on working with plasterboard. Installing the door casing and the door itself is discussed in the section on hanging a door.

Turning a Corner

Suppose you're building a wall or a closet and you have to turn a corner. You make the corner out of three studs nailed in place like this:

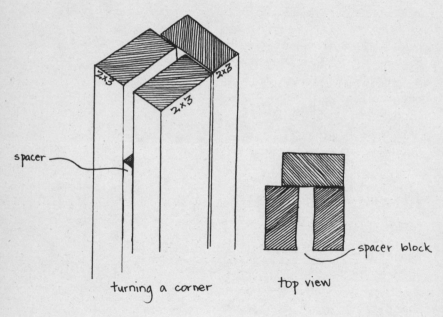

turning a corner   top view

This construction gives you something to nail your plaster-board into on both the front and the back of your partition. The two parallel studs are kept apart with spacers of 1″ or 2 x 3 scrap. If you don't space these studs, you won't have much to nail your plasterboard to on the inside of your corner, and you may run into problems.

Other Wall-Building Advice

You will read other ways of building partitions in other books, for example, nailing the sole plate down, then cutting and measuring all your studs, nailing them to the top plate, lifting the whole thing into place on top of the sole plate, and nailing it into position. Or even building the whole partition on the floor as an entire unit, lifting it into place, then nailing the top and bottom of it into the floor and ceiling. In new construction, okay, but I wouldn't try these methods in an old place. There are so many irregularities in the ceilings and floors that you're sure to find spots where things are too tight and you have to chop away at the plaster, and other spots where the top plate hits nothing but air and you have to shim (see glossary) like mad.

You will also read that you should nail the sole plate down as one piece and saw out the door opening later. This lets you line up the plate on the sides of the doorway very nicely, but you have to be better than I am to avoid cutting into the floor when you do your sawing.

REMOVING A PARTITION

The kind of partition we've just built is non-load-bearing: that is, as you probably will remember, it doesn't help hold the house up. Most partitions are of this type, and you can tear out as many of them as you like. But sometimes a partition *is* load-bearing. You can't remove one of these without a lot of trouble and expense. You have to replace them with another bearing member, sometimes a steel beam. Before you buy a place you'd better know which partitions, if any, are load-bearing —or a lot of your remodeling plans can go down the drain.

Knowing which partitions are which isn't always easy. The outside walls of houses are load-bearing. But in some old places, especially city houses made of brick, the current back of the house has been *added* to the original structure. From within the home you enter this addition by means of a doorway chopped through what used to be the rear wall of the building. The original rear wall has become an interior partition.

Watch out for this one. I ran into plenty of houses like this in Philadelphia. You walk into the place, see a small living room, a tiny dining room, then a doorway leading to a kitchen in the rear. You think: We'll just wipe out all these walls and have one great big room with a pullman kitchen. But that wall between the dining room and the kitchen is a load-bearing wall and consists of a couple of layers ("courses") of brick. Tearing it out and replacing its function with a beam is a major engineering job. So unless you have buckets of money, you are going to have to live with that wall. You can usually identify such a load-bearing wall just by banging on it: it will sound and feel very different from a partition made of studs and plaster. Solid. Also, its doorjamb (the side and top lining of the doorway) will be much thicker than the other doorjambs in the house.

Except for walls like these, you will usually be able to tear out all the partitions in a city row house. The floor joists in most city houses run across the entire width of the house from party wall to party wall. (Party walls are the brick load-bearing walls that separate one row house from another.) Since the floor joists rest on these bearing walls, you will most often be able to knock out all the partitions under them without fear that the floors will fall in.

Still, load-bearing walls take some tricky forms, and you have to be very careful. In some larger row houses, for example, you may find an inner-bearing partition—often a hallway wall. So be careful.

If you have any doubts, by all means check things out before you start bashing. Your home inspection service should give you the information you need. If you know an engineer or architect or builder, have one of them look at the partition. Check with

the neighbors. See if anyone else with a similar house has ripped
out the wall you'd like to get rid of.

A bearing wall almost always runs across the joists, not
parallel to them. But if your city row house has been chopped up
by previous owners, someone may have done some crazy thing
that made it necessary to run a bearing wall in the same
direction the joists run. Admittedly, this is an unusual situation.
But it could happen. Here is an example:

When we started work on Lambert Street we were faced with
the following: what had once been the dining room had been
divided into a large closet, a small room intended as a powder
room but never finished, and a stairway. This new stairway ran
into the back room on the second floor, which had been sealed
off from the upstairs hallway. This was too weird for us, and we
set about restoring the area to its original layout. I tore out the
powder room and closet, was about to tear out the stairway
when a curious premonition overcame me.

Inspecting things cautiously, I found that the previous owner
had cut out three-foot sections from five of the second floor
joists in order to install his stairway. The longer sections of these
cut-off joists were now held up by the downstairs hallway wall.
The shorter sections came out of the party wall about six feet
and just hung there, held up by nothing but force of habit. Not
only this, but these cut-off joists were in the second floor
kitchen—right under the refrigerator.

In a way it was reassuring to see these hanging joists holding
up a refrigerator. I figured no matter what I did to the place, I
couldn't come up with anything as bad as that. And it was nice
to know that even butchery that bad hadn't sent the place
tumbling down. Such a situation, however, would've been
uncomfortable to live with. Dick, our carpenter, bridged three of
the cut-off joists with some timber I found in the cellar, tied two
others together with a header (see glossary), and then in the
room below built a 4 x 4 bearing wall for added support.
Fortunately we were able to put this wall in a spot where we

needed a partition anyway. The end result was that the partition ran parallel to the joists.

You could probably tear this particular wall out and still be okay, because Dick did a fine job of repairing the mangled joists, but in some old places you are undoubtedly going to have walls like this that you can't tear out. They are just about impossible to detect. Fortunately, they are also quite rare.

In a house that stands by itself, a non-row house, you are quite likely to run into an inner-bearing wall. Always check anything that runs at right angles to the floor joists before you lay a hand on it.

Okay. Unless you are gutting your old place, you're not likely to tear out more than a couple of inside walls. (If you *are* gutting it, you are likely to have an architect or a builder working with you who will—usually—be able to tell you what can and what can't be torn out.) With walls, the things most do-it-yourselfers will try are: removing a wall between rooms in order to make a bigger room, and ripping out old closets. You're on pretty safe ground here. Walls between rooms are usually not bearing, and I *never* heard of a bearing closet. (I am sure, however, that somewhere one exists.)

On Lawrence Street we tore out the partition between the living and dining rooms and made one beautiful large bright room. It was obvious that this wall was not structural—because when you pushed on the doorjamb, the whole partition swayed back and forth. I hope the walls that you want to tear out are in similar shape.

Before you smash, find out if pipes and wires run through your wall. Wires can be run somewhere else fairly easily, but changing pipe runs is costly, and if you have a wall full of pipes, think twice before touching it. If you're not sure what's inside your partition, take it apart *carefully*.

If you've never torn out a plaster wall before, you won't believe the amount of rubbish you'll be stuck with. The wall on Lawrence Street was the first one I'd ever demolished. It came down quickly, but it filled twenty-five good-sized boxes with plaster and lath. We put them out on the sidewalk, cursing the drizzle, cringing when the trash collectors came. They took them all. (It was Christmas-tip time.) We tried the same thing on Lambert Street with a demolished closet (only twelve boxes), but it was September. The doorbell rang and the man looked at me sullenly and said, "We ain't takin' no *see*ment." Fortunately, two dollars changed his mind.

Use your 40 ounce hammer to do the bashing; it'll do a much better job than a regular hammer. It will handle most of the lath and knock the studs out fairly easily too. You'll have to remove some of the lath with your pry bar.

Keep wetting the wall and floor as you work, to hold down the dust. Fill a bucket with water and use a large paint brush to splash the water around—you'll need to keep things pretty wet. Wear gloves, or you'll be full of splinters. Wear a mask if you can stand it. If you're living in the place when you do this job, tack a damp sheet across the doorway to confine the dust to the room you're working in, and open the windows (to suffocate the neighbors). Believe me, plaster dust gets into *everything*.

If the studs are in good shape, hang onto them, you can build a closet or something out of them later. Never get rid of wood unless it's absolutely worthless.

COVERING A PARTITION

Working with Plasterboard

The material most often used to cover partitions nowadays is gypsum wallboard, also called simply wallboard, drywall, plasterboard, or Sheetrock (which is actually a brand name). A friend of mine even called it "dryboard," but I've never heard anyone else call it that, and things are confusing enough as it is. Let's agree to call it plasterboard.

To apply plasterboard to your framing you will need the following materials: hammer, screwdriver, plasterboard nails, utility knife and pocket knife, steel square, yardstick, and keyhole saw.

Plasterboard consists of gypsum plaster sandwiched between two layers of heavy paper. For the most part, it comes in $\frac{3}{8}''$, $\frac{1}{2}''$, and $\frac{5}{8}''$ thicknesses.* (There is a $\frac{1}{4}''$ thickness used to resurface existing walls, but it's relatively rare.) It comes in sheets that are 4 feet wide and usually either 8, 10 or 12 feet long. The paper on one side of the board is smooth and white or cream-colored. This is the side that faces the room and receives the finish treatment.

The characteristics and quality of plasterboard vary with the manufacturer. The paper will stick to the plaster core better on some boards than on others: With one brand, if you rip the paper backing while removing a piece of board that you've cut off, you'll be right down to the plaster; with another brand you'll simply be down to another layer of paper. The plaster core in some boards will crumble easily: If you accidentally hit the corner of the board on the floor just slightly, you'll break it; other boards hit the same way won't show any damage at all. The finish paper will differ in texture and color from brand to brand. The best plasterboard I've ever used is the National Gypsum Company's Gold Bond.

The ideal partition "skin" would be light, easy to work with and finish, inexpensive, opaque, sound absorbent, and sturdy enough to resist the kids. So far there isn't any such thing. Plasterboard is a compromise, and not a bad one. It's fairly easy to work with and finish, cheap, opaque, and sturdy. It isn't light, though, and its hard surface lets sound right through.

---

* There is also a green-faced plasterboard with a water-repellent surface and water-resistant core. This is known as "M-R" (moisture-resistant) board or waterproof wallboard. This is used around sinks and tubs and as a backing for tiles in shower stalls. It costs about twice as much as the same thickness regular plasterboard.

Years ago I used to dislike plasterboard. It seemed flimsy and far inferior to plaster and lath. That was in the days when nearly all plasterboard was ⅜″ thick. (It was also before I'd ever worked with the stuff.) Nowadays the ½″ thickness is used most frequently—and what a difference. The increase in solidity created by that extra ⅛″ is incredible.

Actually, ⅜″ plasterboard is plenty strong enough for a partition. But if you feel the need for something quite substantial, or feel embarrassed as your walls quiver when punched by friends who know you've done it yourself, go with the ½″ stuff. It won't cost you much more than the ⅜″—there is very little difference in price between the two thicknesses. However there is *quite* a difference in their weight, and therefore in their ease of handling. An 8 foot sheet of ½″ plasterboard is tough for one person to manipulate, much tougher than an 8 foot sheet of ⅜″. So for the insides of closets and other hidden places where your friends won't pound, by all means use the ⅜″. As for the ⅝″ stuff, don't mess with it unless you're a masochist.

It's also best to stick with the standard 8 foot lengths when you're doing the job alone. The 10 foot lengths are really unwieldy. I once bought 10 foot long ⅜″ sheets to do the inside walls of my Lambert Street study. I figured the longer stuff would reduce the number of seams in the finished wall. It did. But a few extra seams would've been nothing compared to the struggle I had with that stuff in that tiny room.

Covering the inside of exterior walls is a slightly different matter. If you're furring out the exterior walls (attaching wood strips to them) of an old *brick* house and re-covering them, go ahead and use ⅜″ plasterboard. But if you're finishing the exterior walls of an old *frame* house, use the ½″ material, for two good reasons: One, since it's stronger than the thinner stuff, it will help to brace these outside walls. And two, it will give you better fire protection than the thinner material. These qualities are not important when you're dealing with brick walls, but they're very important when you're dealing with frame construction.

A note on the fire rating of plasterboard: the rating increases with the board's thickness. The ½″ or thicker material is labeled "fire resistant." Try to burn a piece sometime. Turn up your propane torch full blast and hold it close to the plasterboard for several minutes. The paper facing will burn away and the core will glow orange, but when you turn off the torch, the back of the board will be barely warm. Plaster gives off water when heated. This process is called calcination. It increases the plasterboard's fire resistance. It also makes the board fall apart. Calcination begins very slowly between 110 and 125 degrees F. and increases at temperatures higher than this. So while the plasterboard won't burn, it will deteriorate if exposed to high heat for any length of time. That's why you can't put a free-standing fireplace right next to it. And after a long time, if the fireplace is very close, enough heat can get through the plasterboard to allow the studs behind it to burn.

To cut plasterboard you score the finish paper—that is, the smooth, white side—with your utility knife. You don't have to cut deeply into the plaster; as long as you get through the paper facing, you're okay. A steel yardstick is a good guide for the knife, it won't slide as much as a wooden one and won't get cut up along with the plasterboard. An even better straightedge is a length of plasterboard a few inches wide. (A wooden board isn't so good; you'll gouge it with your knife and your scoring won't be straight.)

Plasterboard is easiest to cut when it's flat on the floor, but you can also cut it when it's standing up. After I score the surface, if the piece I'm cutting off is a foot or so wide, I like to stand the board up with the uncut (gray) side facing me and rest it on my shoe. My foot keeps the edge of the board off the floor, and the part of the board that I want to break off hangs in the air. I hit this free piece sharply with my open hand, snapping the plaster core. I then rest the board on the floor again and slice through the gray paper backing with my utility knife. If you're cutting off a larger piece, you can usually stand it up and snap it without having to rest it on your foot.

When you're taking off less than a 6″ piece or are taking a piece off the long side of the board, cut the board on the floor, then put a 2 x 4 or other thick straightedge under the cut and sharply smack the part to be removed. Then pick the board up and cut through the gray paper from the back. Always use a very sharp blade to do this work. (A utility knife blade can be sharpened with your stone a few times. You don't have to reverse it or toss it away every time it gets dull.)

It's kind of troublesome to cut off a long thin piece of plasterboard, let's say 1½″ wide or less. Unless you score the board on both the front *and* the back, you'll often find that the board won't snap off cleanly, and the edge may crumble. The easiest way to cut off thin pieces like these is to score the surface just as if you were going to snap the piece off (or maybe a little more heavily), and then saw the piece off with your keyhole saw. The scoring provides a guide for the saw blade to follow, and the saw cut will give you a clean, uncrumbled edge.

You will have to cut holes in the plasterboard for light switches, outlets, etc. There are two main ways of doing this. Take a pencil and draw the area to be cut out on the face of the plasterboard. In method one, bore holes in the corners of this drawing with a screwdriver, then cut out the piece with your keyhole saw. In method two, score around the outline with your utility knife, then score an "X" across the middle of it from corner to corner. Tap the middle of the X with your hammer, breaking through the board. Then cut the gray backing with your knife. This second method is quicker, but it gives you more ragged results than the first.

How can you make sure to cut these holes in the right spots in the plasterboard? Time and again I've read that the way to mark your cutouts on the board is this: Take a piece of carpenter's chalk (usually a light blue) and rub it along the edge of the electrical outlet or junction box. Then hold your plasterboard in place against the wall and bang on it in the area of the outlet box. The chalk outline of the box will be transferred to the gray paper backing and you're set. But it never seems to work that way for me. Sometimes I get one blue line, occasionally a corner, but never the whole thing. Also, the protruding outlet box keeps you from fitting your plasterboard tightly up against the wall, and when you bang the board it's likely to slip. The idea sounds great and it ought to work, but I've given up on it.

Instead I just measure the location of the box: up from the floor and in from the closest wall (or edge of the next piece of plasterboard). This gives me the location of either the right or left lower corner of the box. I transfer this measurement to the plasterboard, then take an outlet or junction box identical with the one in the wall, put its corner on the corner I've marked on the board, and trace around it. (Instead of using the actual box you can make a cardboard template of the box.) Cut your opening a little bigger than this tracing. This procedure doesn't seem to take any longer than the blue chalk method, and it always works out better for me. No matter which method you use, unless you are super you will probably find that your cutout's a little bit off when you put the board up to the wall again. Okay, you're only human. Most of these discrepancies will be covered by the outlet plate or fixture. Others you'll have to fill with joint cement (coming up shortly). Take your time in measuring and cutting and you'll minimize these mistakes.

Plasterboard manufacturers suggest that you apply their product horizontally, the long way across the studs. The material is supposed to make the wall stronger when it's applied like this, and you're also supposed to end up with fewer seams. I would add another reason to these. While you can apply the material vertically, the long way running from floor to ceiling, you'll probably find this more awkward, especially when you're trying to maneuver an electrical box into a cutout you've made for it.

Beyond this, it's best to use plasterboard vertically only when your studs are 16″ or 24″ on center. When your studs are spaced like this, you have an even 4 foot span over which to nail the board. But in most old places the old studs are not 16″ or 24″ on center. The first few studs on the wall facing me as I write this are spaced this way: 18″, 16″, 16″, 17″, 15″, 9″. It is 7 feet, 9″ from the corner stud to the center of the stud at the end of this span. I can apply two 8 foot sheets of plasterboard horizontally here, one above the other, with only 3″ (x 8 feet) of waste. If I applied the plasterboard vertically, I could cover only the first three studs, a span of 40″, with my first board. (You have to nail the edge of the board into a stud, you can't let an edge hang out unsupported beyond a stud.) So here I'd have to cut 8″ off the board, and I'd waste 8″ x 8 feet of material. My next sheet, extending to the center of the 9″ stud, would take me only 41″ farther. So here I'd lose another 7″ x 8 feet of material. With the horizontal method I'd have 288 square inches of waste. The vertical method would give me 1,440 square inches of waste. So in old places with their random studs, you'd better stick to the horizontal.

Blue Nails

To secure the plasterboard to the framing, you use a special nail usually called a drywall nail or "blue nail" in hardware stores and lumberyards. They're called blue nails because the most common type has a gunmetal blueblack finish. But other drywall nails don't. Some have the same shiny finish as a regular nail and some are galvanized. You can use any of these. The important differences among drywall nails are their length and whether or not they have a ringed shank.

When working with ½″ plasterboard, you'll want to use ringed shank blue nails 1¼″ long or longer. In the ceiling it's better to use 1⅜″ or 1½″ nails, but you often can't find a store that carries them. Sometimes your local supply won't have any ringed nails, but keep searching. They hold much better than the plain-shank nails. On ceilings, that's especially important.

You should have a small supply of 1 ¼" smooth-shank nails on hand too, so pick up a pound. Sometimes there are spots that a ringed nail just won't penetrate—such as a springy piece of furring—or sometimes you'll need to patch a spot with a very small piece of plasterboard, and the smooth-shank nails are great for securing such small stuff. They come in handy on the ceiling, too, as I'll explain.

You drive blue nails in just slightly below the surface of the plasterboard. The hammer should dent the board. But don't drive the nails in so hard that they break the board's paper covering, or the board will pop out around them. With the better quality boards it's easy to "dimple" the surface like this, but with the poorer ones you really have to be careful. Make the last hammer blow a gentle one.

The Problem of Ceilings

If you have any ceilings to cover with plasterboard, in principle you're supposed to get them up before you cover your walls. You do this so that the plasterboard on the walls will come up under the edges of the plasterboard on the ceiling and help hold it in place. This is fine but not essential, as far as I'm concerned, if you use enough long, ringed shank nails to attach the ceiling plasterboard. But since the ceiling is, quite literally, a pain in the neck to cover, let's get it out of the way right now.

How do you apply plasterboard to a ceiling? I have before me a brochure that shows you. The illustrated man and wife perform the task with amazing ease, smiling all the while. Sure.

Go ahead, I dare you—just try to smile while supporting a piece of plasterboard over your head. Even the smaller pieces are fantastically awkward and heavy. An 8 foot sheet of ⅜" stuff is brutal for two people to handle and the ½" stuff is just about impossible. If you have to try to make it fit over an electrical box in the ceiling, oh boy.

I've given up trying to work with the full-size sheets overhead. I cut them in half. I know that gives you another seam to finish, but to me it's better than a back spasm. Because of the crazy spacing of rafters in old places you can sometimes use a piece a little longer than 4 feet, but for me 5 feet is the limit.

Installing plasterboard on the ceiling is a job for at least two people. One person gets up on a stepladder (or a sturdy table or box, if it's high enough) and holds one end of the plasterboard while simultaneously driving in nails to secure it to the ceiling. The person doing the nailing obviously gets the short end of this deal. Once the plasterboard is in place, this person has to hold it there and nail it into the joists or rafters. This means he (or she) has to hold up the board with the same hand that holds the nail.

The other person stays on the ground and supports the other end of the material with some sort of brace. The things I've read say to take a piece of lumber slightly longer than the floor-to-ceiling height of the room you're working in and nail a piece of wood across the top to form a "T." You then stick the "T" end of this brace under the plasterboard and wedge the other end into the floor. Thus the floor bears a lot of the board's weight. I've found two things wrong with this: You really have to make that T brace strong, or it will soon fall apart under the weight of the plasterboard. And the length of this type of brace makes it hard to maneuver, especially in a small room.

The best brace I've found is a garden rake; it's extremely sturdy and since the tines are a little rough, they don't slip off the plasterboard readily. Not quite as good, but serviceable, is a push broom. If you work with 4 foot sections of material instead of 8 foot sections, you will find that the weight is not so great that you have to rest the end of the rake or broom on the floor.

Nailing plasterboard overhead has to be one of the best arm exercises in the world. Occasionally in emergencies I have resorted to supporting the plasterboard with my head. This forces your larynx into your breastbone, and for a day or so afterward you talk like Donald Duck. If you have naked studs on your walls, try this: nail a piece of scrap wood across the top of a few of the studs, about 1″ down from the ceiling. (Don't drive the nails in all the way, you'll want to remove them later.) Rest the end of the plasterboard on this cleat. Then you can give your arms a rest before you pick up your hammer and nail and go at it. If things don't work out right, you rest the board on the cleat again instead of letting it smash you to the floor. Once you've put in enough nails to hold the board in place, you can remove the cleat.

It doesn't take many nails to hold the plasterboard up temporarily. But you'll want to get even these few nails in as fast as possible to minimize the chances of dislocating your arms. I like to use the smooth-shank nails for this initial step. Ringed nails are harder to drive than smooth-shank nails, and harder to drive into ceilings than into walls, and this is one time when you don't want to fool around. Once you've driven in 5 or 6 smooth nails and have the board in place, you can relax and secure it for keeps with the longest ringed nails you can find.

You're supposed to nail from the center of the plasterboard out toward the edges. This insures that the board will contact the framing evenly, with no bulges. Sometimes you won't find it possible to nail this way. I'm just happy to get the thing up there, and I nail any way I can. So far I haven't had any problems.

Manufacturers recommend placing nails no more than 7″ apart on ceilings. You might want to nail at intervals a few inches wider than this but use two nails at each spot instead of only one. This double-nailing method will prevent nails from popping out later on. (Or so they say, and they're probably right. I use this method all the time now, and so far, no popping.) You're not supposed to nail closer than ⅜″ to the edge of a sheet. If you do, the edge may crumble.

The addition of a third party to this ceiling operation makes it about ten times easier. If it happens to be a very strong third party, you might even want to tackle a full-size sheet of plasterboard. Maybe.

Walls

After the ceiling is in place you are supposed to do the upper section of the walls. This lets you get the plasterboard nice and snug against the ceiling pieces, giving them support around the edges. As I say, I've never had any trouble doing it the other way around. In any case, if you go by the standard rules, you should put the wall's upper piece in place first, to get the snug fit. But if you're doing the walls alone or even with one other person, you're going to find it tough sledding to keep that upper board in place while you're trying to drive nails into it. So, again, I regularly depart from the recommended procedure. I almost always do the bottom board first.

Before you put your plasterboard on the wall, take your pencil and, on both the floor and ceiling, mark the location of the center of each stud you're going to cover up. Then when you put your board up you'll remember just where each stud is. If you don't make these marks, your blue nails may hit nothing but air.

Never jam the edges of plasterboard pieces together; they should meet, but not be compressed. You should also leave a little space between the floor and the lower edge of the bottom piece of plasterboard to allow for expansion. I take a strip of ¼" plywood or a piece of wood lath and put it on the floor in the center of the spot where the plasterboard is to go. I rest the board on the wood, position the board, and drive a couple of nails into its top. Then I remove the lath or plywood and I have my expansion space. Don't drive a whole lot of nails into the plasterboard before you take the wood strip out, or you won't ever *get* it out. Once you've removed the wood strip, drive in the rest of your nails, nailing from the center out and spacing the nails no more than 8" apart (unless you use the double-nailing method).

Once the lower plasterboard pieces are in place, I rest the upper pieces on top of them and nail them in. Having the lower boards as support makes the job a lot easier.

Holes, Seams, and Joint Cement

After all the plasterboard's up, you'll be faced with a whole bunch of seams to finish and hundreds of nails to cover. You do this job with joint cement, one of man's great inventions.

There are two basic types of joint cement, the powdered kind (smallest size is usually 5 pounds) and the ready-mixed, which often contains vinyl (smallest size is usually 1 gallon). Either kind will do. The ready-mixed is certainly less trouble, but in small quantities it's more expensive than the powdered kind. But you'll probably need more than 5 pounds anyway. You can save money on the ready-mixed by buying it in 5 gallon buckets. Five gallons seems like a lot, but it goes fast, and if you're doing a whole room, by all means buy it in this larger size.

There are several very nice things about joint cement. It is sticky and readily clings to the wall. It is easy to smooth out and can be spread to a feather edge. And it sets up slowly; you don't have to rush your job. Once it's on the wall it takes about a day to dry to the point where you can sand it. (If you're in a hurry, there's a special kind that dries completely in less than 3 hours.) The mixed up, powdered kind will stay workable for days if you keep it in a closed container. The ready-mixed stays good for months.

Now I once heard a guy from a prefab housing firm tell his radio interviewer that finishing plasterboard seams was one job he did not recommend for do-it-yourselfers. To me this is crazy. There is no reason why any ordinary person can't do this job. He will have to take more time than the professional, but he will probably come out with at least as good a job if he's careful. Of course a guy who does just drywall work is very, very good, and you won't beat him. But jack-of-all-trades contractors often slack off on this part of the job. It's one of the last things they do, they're ready to finish up and get on to someone else's place, and they get it out of the way as fast as they can. Very often they ignore all the rules: they use plain shank nails, use too few of them, set them too deep, etc. I've seen professional work where not only the seams but the actual joints between the sheets of plasterboard were still visible when the job was "done." You could see where most of the nails were, too. True, this makes it handy when you want to find a stud to hang a picture on, but first class it isn't.

Here are the materials you'll need to patch the seams in your plasterboard: joint cement, joint tape, taping knives, 3″ putty knife, bucket of water and medium-size cellulose sponge, coarse and fine sandpaper. Joint tape is paper with tiny holes in it that make it adhere to the joint cement. You'll see how it works in a minute.

You'll want two different kinds of taping knives. One kind looks like a big putty knife, but it's more flexible. You can get these up to 8″ wide, but many people find the big ones tough to handle. I'd get one 4″ wide. The other knife looks like a plasterer's trowel with a slightly bowed blade. It is about 9″ long by 6″ wide.

You apply joint cement in four steps.

Step 1. The long edges of plasterboard sheets are tapered. So, where the long edges of two sheets butt together, they form a slight depression that's about 2″ wide on each side of the joint, or a total of 4″ wide. Scoop up some cement on the end of your 4″ taping knife and press it into the joint, spreading it out so it fills the entire 4″ wide depression. Do this along the whole seam. The band of cement should be about ⅛″ thick.

Next take a piece of tape the length of the seam (cut the tape if you're neat, tear it off if you're like I am), and press it on top of the cemented seam with your fingers. Then go over the tape with your knife, pressing it well into the cement and scraping off any excess. You should cover the tape with a very thin coat of the cement. Get the cement as smooth as you can and don't leave any big lumps sticking out. It won't be a tragedy if you do, but you'll make the next step easier if you don't.

While the long edges of plasterboard sheets are tapered, the short edges (the 4-foot-long ends) are not. And sometimes you'll have to cut off a tapered edge to get a sheet to fit a certain space. So there will be times when a tapered edge meets an untapered edge, or when two untapered edges meet. What then?

Instructions in company brochures and home repair books are strangely silent on this point. Well, I don't do anything different from what I do when I join two tapered edges. I've found that as long as you spread the cement out wide enough, you can barely see the seam even though you're working with an untapered edge. If you are very critical and think you'll notice the seam, you can do what some guys I hired once did with endless hours of my time and money while I was off at work: peel away the paper facing on both sides of the seam. You cut the paper along the seam about 2″ from the edge on both sides and just peel it away. This gives you your groove to fill. As far as I'm concerned it's a waste of time. The seams I did without using this technique turned out better than the seams they did using it.

Once you've applied the cement, you have to let the area dry completely (until the next day, if you're using the standard compound) before you go on to step 2—which is to cover the seam again with another coat of cement.

Step 2. If you've left any lumps of cement sticking up, scrape them off with a wood chisel. Now you're ready to use the trowel-like knife, the one that's 9″ long by 6″ wide, with a slightly bowed blade. Apply the cement with the broad side of the blade. Put a lot of cement on the edge of the blade, then pull the knife across the seam, applying pressure as evenly as you can. Use both hands. The bowed blade is designed to give you a tapered seam, thicker in the center than at the edges. It's easier to taper the seam with this type of tool than with the putty knife type because you get a 9″ wide band of cement on the wall in one operation.

If your hands are small, you may find this method awkward. If so, you'll have to do this second coat with the narrow edge of this trowel. (Be sure to spread the cement out 9″ or so wide.) You'll have to do some smoothing with this narrow edge anyway. I find it smooths better than the 4″ knife.

Let the seam set up for a few hours until it's fairly firm. Then take your damp sponge and wipe it along the length of the seam, smoothing the cement out as much as you can. The smoother you get it now, the less you will have to sand later. If the seam is too soft, you might not get good results unless you're very careful, so give it time to firm up. If the seam has dried out a lot, you'll have to have your sponge pretty wet.

Step 3. When the seam has dried completely (give it till at least the next day), take a good look at it. If it still looks lumpy, don't worry. Wet the seam with the sponge again, then scrape the high spots off with your 3″ putty knife. The blade will peel off thin pieces of the joint cement. Rub over the joint with the sponge again, smoothing it still further. Davene developed this scraping and rubbing treatment and it's great. It will work even if the seam's been dry for weeks. Try as hard as you can to get things smooth with the knife and sponge to save yourself sanding work. Joint cement is easier to sand than plaster, but it's still a job, and it makes a fantastic amount of dust.

Step 4. Let things dry overnight again and sand the seam. If you've done a good job with your knife and sponge, you can use the fine sandpaper. If you didn't do such a wonderful job, sand the seam with coarse sandpaper first, then use the fine. Wear gloves, and use either garnet or aluminum oxide paper, not the regular flint paper. An electrical orbital sander does a very smooth job, and saves a lot of work. After your sanding is finished, wipe the joints lightly with a damp sponge to take off the dust that's left on the walls.

A tip: do steps 3 and 4 in *artificial* light. Daylight is so diffuse, it hides irregularities.

That's it—except for corners.

Corners and Trim

You won't be able to use the trowel-type knife in corners (unless you use the narrow end), so you'll have to work with the 4″ joint knife or 3″ putty knife.

Coat your inside corners with cement, crease some tape in the center lengthwise, embed the tape in the cement and smooth over it with the knife. When this coat dries, apply the second, let it set, stick the edge of your damp sponge in the corner, and smooth the joint off.

You cover outside corners with a special metal edging called "corner bead." This is nailed in place through the plasterboard and into the stud beneath. (Smooth-shank nails work fine for this.) Then the edges of the bead are covered with two coats of cement. You don't need any tape. This bead makes a nice straight edge and keeps the corner from breaking if it gets hit with something.

There is also a "casing bead" that you can buy for a neat finish around doors and windows. It isn't essential, but it's nice. Again cover nail holes with two layers of joint cement, allowing the first to dry before you apply the second. Since these areas are small and you don't use any tape, you can usually get them quite smooth. Let them dry *completely,* then rub over them with a damp sponge. This should smooth them out nicely without any sanding. (No dust!)

REPAIRING PLASTER WALLS AND CEILINGS

Partitions in old places were usually covered with plaster. Strips of wood, called lath, were nailed onto the studs or other partition framing, and the plaster was applied in several layers on top of these strips. First came one or two layers of base coat plaster, a heavy, rough material which was sometimes brown and which, years ago, sometimes contained horse hair. (So if you find hair coming out of your walls, you'll know what it is.) Over the base coat went the finish coat, a smooth, white, hard material.

While interior partitions were nearly always built like this, exterior walls in masonry houses (especially houses built before the Civil War) often had no lath; the plaster was applied directly to the brick or stone. Later it became common practice to fur out the walls—that is, to nail wood strips to the masonry and then proceed with lath and plaster just as on interior partitions. This was an improvement: the resulting air space provided some insulation, and it also protected the plaster a bit from moisture that might seep through the brick or stone.

Plaster walls are still being built, but today you're likely to find them mainly in commercial or institutional construction because they cost a fortune compared with plasterboard. They take a lot of time and skill to put together. Today the lath is usually wire mesh or a gypsum board that looks a lot like plasterboard. (People who have this gypsum lath in their homes sometimes think that the builders plastered their plasterboard.)

Cracks

You'll find cracks in any old plaster wall (and in many new ones, too). They range from tiny "hairline" cracks to exterior wall cracks ½" wide or wider, several feet long and deeper than you'd believe possible.

Unless a crack is really tiny, you'll have to bridge it with something. Because unless it's tiny, if you simply fill it with patching material, it is almost certain to open up again sometime. This is especially true in city houses. Trucks and cars and buses keep the city house in motion. A repair that isn't bridged doesn't stand a chance.

The easiest way to fix a hairline crack is to use vinyl spackle paste. This is ready mixed, comes in a can, and can be bought in hardware stores, paint stores, and building supply houses. In addition to the spackle you will need a putty knife, a beer can opener or old screwdriver, and some sort of tape. The best tape I've found for the purpose is rubberized crack-patching tape. You can buy it at Sears. There are some three hundred and fifty different kinds of tape on the market and you might find something else that's suitable, but this stuff is made for the job.

If the crack is really tiny and the plaster around it is sound, just scoop up a little spackle on your putty knife, press it firmly into the crack, and smooth it off. It has a nice consistency and is easy to smooth. But be sure to get the excess off the wall, because this stuff sets up very hard and you don't want to have to do a lot of sanding. And be sure to close the can tightly when you're through, or the spackle will dry out and get lumpy.

If the crack is between $\frac{1}{16}''$ and $\frac{1}{8}''$ wide, use the tape. First scrape out the crack with the beer can opener and brush or blow away the dust. (Sometimes what appears to be a hairline crack turns out to be a whopper once you've scraped it.) Fill the crack as above, then take a piece of rubberized tape of sufficient length and cover it. Don't soak the gummed surface of the tape so much that it won't stick. Press the tape firmly over the crack and let it dry. When it's dry, spread a thin coat of spackle over it with the putty knife. When that dries, sand very lightly with fine sandpaper.

This makes a very nice repair. The rubberized tape is so thin that on some occasions I haven't even bothered to cover it with spackle. Once it was painted, it was almost impossible to detect.

When your cracks are wider than $\frac{1}{8}''$, or when they are any depth at all, the vinyl spackle won't do—you'll find that it will crack and shrink. For these jobs you'll want to use patching plaster. This comes in powdered form and is mixed with water. One thing you don't want to use is Plaster of Paris. It is hard and strong, but it sets up too fast. It seems you no sooner get it mixed than it starts to harden, and within ten minutes or so you're stuck with a pan of little stones. You can retard the set by mixing some vinegar into your water, but it's best to avoid the stuff except for a special case I'll get to later.

Patching plaster is a mixture of Plaster of Paris and other materials that retard the set and aid ease of application. Powdered spackling compound is almost the same thing, but it usually contains less Plaster of Paris. The ingredients of spackling compound and patching plaster vary according to the manufacturer, and you can't tell what the qualities of the product are until you use it. I once bought some "patching plaster" that looked like glue, set hard as concrete and was practically impossible to sand. If you stick to the stuff manufactured by well-known firms like Gold Bond, USG, UGL, and Sears, you should be okay. Or you can make your own patching plaster by mixing Plaster of Paris half and half with joint cement. This isn't a bad idea, because you may need a bit of Plaster of Paris for something, and you'll almost certainly need some joint cement, so this way you'll have them on hand as well as a reliable patching plaster.

Okay, let's suppose you have a nice big crack ½" wide by 4 feet long. How do you go about fixing it?

Take your beer can opener and scrape any crumbling plaster away from the edge of the crack. You may find some pieces of plaster an inch or so wide that look like they might fall off with a little encouragement. Don't encourage them. The way we're going to fix this crack, they'll be all right when the job is done.

Clean the crack with a dustbrush or old paint brush. If it's full of dirt, vacuum it out. The instructions on most patching plaster boxes say to get the crack absolutely clean, but that's impossible. Just do the best you can.

Once the crack is reasonably clean, soak it thoroughly with water. If you don't, the dry old wall will suck the water out of your plaster and it won't set up right. You can use an old squeeze bottle for this job, the kind detergents come in, or a water pistol. The water pistol holds less and gives a finer spray, but for some of you it may make the job more fun, and anything that makes the job more fun is worth it.

You don't want to end up throwing pounds of plaster into the gap, so if the crack is very deep and is in a brick or stone wall, fill it up with something before you patch. Old newspaper works fine. Wet it, crumple it up, and stuff it in the hole with an old screwdriver or stick. For a stronger, water-resistant filler, you can use sand or mortar mix (see the section later in this chapter on ready-mix cement). Don't use concrete mix (cement with stones in it), because most of the stones in the mix will be too big to fit into the crack. (If the crack is in an interior partition, you omit this step, the lath serves as a backing for your patch.)

Once you've got the filler to within ½″ of the wall surface, mix enough plaster to fill the crack the rest of the way. (Don't ask me how you can figure out how much to use; you just guess.) You always mix plaster (or joint cement or powdered spackle) by putting some water in a container and then sprinkling the powder over it. Start with just a little water, or you may end up using most of your box of plaster to get the mix thick enough. The box will usually tell you the proper proportions of plaster and water. I'd go light on the water.

The finished mix should be just a little looser than toothpaste. Scoop some up on the edge of your 3″ putty knife and press it into the hole. (Use your fingers if it's easier.) Fill the whole crack until it's flush with the surrounding plaster. Smooth it off as well as you can.

The next day, when the plaster is dry (or pretty dry), bridge and finish off the crack. You can use the rubberized tape and vinyl spackle to do this, but a better and less expensive way is to use joint cement and tape. Treat the crack exactly as you would a joint in plasterboard, applying a layer of joint cement and tape, then a finish layer of cement. This will keep the crack from opening again, and stick those loose and crumbly parts around its edge together firmly. For extra strength you can use two layers of tape.

This method will give you a very nice-looking repair that will hold up far better than patching plaster alone. But be sure to use patching plaster as your filler. Joint cement is not terribly strong, and it will shrink and crack if you use it to fill deep gaps.

Breaks and Holes

You will likely find places in your house where plaster has fallen off the lath. Sometimes a leak has weakened the plaster, sometimes someone has hit it with something. Some old places have been empty for a winter or two; the contraction of the walls by the cold has made the plaster break and fall away.

Sometimes only the finish coat of plaster has been damaged and the base coat is still sound. If this is the case, scrape and brush all loose material away from the break, then take your beer can opener and bevel the edge of the break so it's deeper on the inside than it is on the outside. This will give the new plaster a notch to cling to. For this kind of repair, a small pointing trowel or plasterer's trowel is easier to use than a large putty knife.

After the hole is clean, mix up a batch of plaster with your trowel. Wet the hole thoroughly with your squeeze bottle, then trowel the plaster over the hole, bringing it out almost but not quite flush with the rest of the wall. (About $\frac{1}{8}''$ from the surface is good.) Get the plaster as smooth as you can and let it dry overnight. The next day, mix up more plaster, making the mix a little looser than before, wet the patch again, and trowel the new plaster over it. If you're really good, you'll be able to get this coat so smooth that after it dries you'll only need to give it a light sanding. But troweling plaster smooth takes practice. If you have trouble with it, once you've done the best you can, take an old paintbrush, wet it a little and go over the patch with even strokes. This will make it look pretty good. When it's dry you can sand away the brush marks.

An alternative is to do the best you can with the trowel, let the patch dry, then the following day sand down any high spots and spread a thin coat of joint cement over the area with your 3″ putty knife or taping knife. Later you can sponge and sand this very smooth. But only use the joint cement for the second coat, not for the whole job. In deep applications it develops multiple fissures and it's hard to smooth out.

Deep Breaks

Suppose both the finish and base coats of plaster have fallen off the wall and you've got a bunch of wood strips staring at you.

If the hole is relatively small (a foot or less in diameter), you can, with some difficulty, fix it in the manner described above. The problem is that if you try to apply patching plaster to the wood lath, you'll probably find yourself losing most of it through the spaces between the strips. A better bet is to apply a coat of perlite plaster (see the sections on flaking, peeling, and crumbling due to dampness, and on perlite, in a few pages), let it dry, and then proceed with the patching plaster steps.

It's quite a trick to create an even, smooth plaster patch over an area larger than a foot in diameter. Rather than try it, take a hammer and cold chisel (see glossary) and widen the damaged area until you can see a stud at both the left and right sides of the hole. Maybe your hole is located directly over a stud. In this case, chisel to either the right or the left until you come to the next stud. Square off the hole with your hammer and chisel. Don't attempt to remove any of the wood lath, it isn't necessary.

Instead of filling this hole with plaster, fill it with a piece of plasterboard. A 4 x 8 foot sheet of the stuff costs around $3. If you can't get a sheet of 4 x 8 in or on your car, have the guy at the lumberyard cut it up, or take your utility knife along, and if the lumberyard guy looks fierce, cut it up yourself.

One problem: The plasterboard won't be thick enough to

bring the patch out flush with the existing plaster. Measure the thickness of the plaster around the hole. If it's 1″ thick, fine, you use two layers of ½″ plasterboard to fill it. If it's ¾″ thick, you can use two pieces of ⅜″ board. But life rarely works out so neatly, and you will probably have to nail some sort of shims to the studs in order to make your patch come out flush. You can use wood shingles or even pieces of stiff cardboard. You may (unluckily) find that each side of the break has a different thickness of plaster. Even things up as well as you can.

Nail the plasterboard over the wood lath and into the studs. Use ringed sheetrock nails. If your patch is two layers thick, nail each piece up separately. In the second layer, use the biggest nails you can get your hands on. To make the outer layer adhere better, you can coat the back of it with wallboard cement. This comes in tubes that fit into your caulking gun; you can get them at the building supply.

Once the plasterboard is in place, treat the edges with joint cement and tape. You may decide that the finished patch is too smooth compared to the old wall surrounding it. If so, smear some joint cement over the whole thing to give it some texture.

Now don't try to shortcut this procedure and nail the plasterboard patches into the lath alone. Wood lath is springy, the nails will just bounce back at you, and your frustrated hammering will probably bring down more of the wall.

Soft Spots

You're sure to find places where your wall feels weak and soft and very precarious even though there aren't any holes in it. These are spots where the plaster has come loose from the lath.

Small areas like this (again, about a foot across) can be repaired with joint cement and tape. You spread both cement and tape over the soft spot and well into the adjacent sound plaster. In larger areas you'd be better off removing the loose stuff and patching the hole with plasterboard.

You may find whole walls that are soft like this. The only

permanent solution is to tear off all the plaster and lath and re-do the walls with plasterboard. However, there are also less extreme (and less permanent) solutions that will work.

Suppose, for instance, that you have a wall like this in your apartment. You want to keep it from falling into your bed, but you don't want to get into tearing it out and building it up again. We once faced this problem in our old city apartment. The wall in our study trembled when you looked at it. That plaster was in *bad* shape, soft, loose, cracked and crumbling. Someone had told us that texture paint was the thing for old beat-up walls, and not knowing any better, we went out and bought some. We didn't know one kind from another, so we picked out a 25 pound box of the powdered kind at Sears. In our ignorance we hit the right thing. The ready-mixed latex-type texture paints would never have done the job on that wall.

We mixed the paint with water until it was a heavy paste, decided it was the right consistency to hold the wall together, and tried to brush it on. Impossible. So we ended up troweling it on about ¼" thick, stuccoing the wall with it. It was very sticky and went on easily without our having to wet the wall or rough up its surface. We'd intended to do the room with the one box of paint, but we ended up using the whole thing on the one bad wall.

It worked great. It took a couple of days to dry out thoroughly, but when it did, the wall was ten times as solid as before. We only lived in the apartment another year and a half, so we didn't have a chance to see the long range stability of our treatment, but for the time that we were there we had no problems with that wall at all.

This texture paint was like joint cement, but denser, and I guess if you mixed powdered joint cement with less water than usual you could trowel it on, just as we did with this paint, and achieve a similar result. If you wanted to avoid a heavily textured surface, you could try applying several *thin* coats of regular density joint cement with a brush.

It is also possible to nail ¼″ or ⅜″ plasterboard right over the old damaged surface and into the studs—if the wall isn't terribly bulging and irregular, which it usually is—and if you can find the studs. If you use this method, you'll have to move your electrical switch and outlet boxes forward so they're flush with this new surface. This means prying them loose and reattaching them, which is no easy job in an old place. If you're going to live in the house for the rest of your life, okay. In an old apartment, I'd stick with the stucco.

Ceiling Breaks

Whenever you can, repair breaks in ceilings with plasterboard. Little pieces aren't hard to work with overhead, but plaster is murder. The feeling you have when a whole laboriously constructed plaster patch falls smack on the floor as soon as you come down from your ladder is not nice (but it's nicer than the feeling you have when it falls on your head).

Flaking, Peeling, and Crumbling Due to Dampness

In masonry houses, it's common to find areas of flaking, peeling, and crumbling on the inside surface of exterior walls. This kind of thing is caused by water soaking through the masonry and into the plaster, which, you recall, was applied right over the brick or stone in old places. Most water soaking through walls comes up through the ground, and so these bad spots are usually near the floor.

There is, unfortunately, no quick and easy solution to these problems. Sometimes the condition looks minor—just some flaking and bubbling paint—but it's really just as bad as if the plaster were more seriously damaged, and the permanent solution is the same: take off the plaster right down to the brick, stucco the brick with two coats of cement, and then apply your finish plaster.

Believe me, I've tried to get around this. I've stuccoed the outside of the wall and coated it with silicone water repellent. No good. The moisture often comes right up inside the bricks from the ground through capillary action, which we won't go into here, but which is a pain in the neck, and nothing you do to the outside of the wall will stop it.

When the problem was very minor, just some flaking, I tried to get around it by scraping off the flakes and covering the area with acrylic latex paint. Acrylic latex is supposed to let moisture pass right through it without being hurt. On my wall it bubbled. It's also bubbled on the walls of houses done over by a lot of developers. I've seen plenty of flaking walls on town houses "completely renovated" by contractors. It's probably not the moisture alone that's the problem, but the salts and alkalis that come to life when the ancient plaster gets wet. So, sad to say, when you have this kind of problem, you've just gotta take the whole thing down.

Now maybe the wall was wrecked by a roof leak instead of ground moisture, or by the runoff from a broken downspout. These are sources of moisture that you can cure completely. But it's still best to take the wall down to the bricks when you fix it. An old wall that's taken in a lot of water will continue to act like a sponge, and just the rainwater that hits its surface will most likely seep right through.

On Lawrence Street we had huge areas in the dining room and kitchen where the plaster had been wrecked by water coming through the walls. The first thing I did was the cement and silicone treatment outside. It helped a little, but not nearly enough. So I took my hammer and cold chisel and chipped off all the plaster—finish coat and base coat—under the dining room window (it was about 8 feet wide). I wire-brushed the bricks as clean as I could, wet the wall thoroughly, applied two coats of ready-mix cement, and then applied the plaster.

Let's take each step in turn.

Ready-Mix Cement and Perlite Plaster

There are three types of ready-mix cement: mortar mix, sand
mix, and concrete mix. Ready-mix cement is not to be confused
with ready-*mixed* cement, which is delivered by cement truck.
"Ready-mix" means ready to be mixed, not mixed already.
Ready-mix comes in small bags (usually sold in hardware stores)
and in 45 pound and 80 or 90 pound bags (sold in lumberyards
and masonry supply houses). Unless you have a really small
area to do, get at least the 45 pound bag; it won't go far.

Mortar mix contains the greatest proportion of Portland
cement of any of the mixes. This is the gray, powdery stuff that
gets sticky when wet. So mortar mix is your choice when you
want to stucco a wall, because it will stick a lot better than
anything else. Just as with patching plaster, the qualities of these
mixes vary with the manufacturer, and one company's mortar
mix may be almost the same as another company's sand mix.
The best known of the ready-mixes is Sakrete, and its mortar
mix is fine for stuccoing.

To mix a substantial amount of mortar, you'll need a mixing
box. You can easily make one with four boards for sides and a
piece of plywood for a bottom. Put it together as tightly as you
can so that it doesn't leak too much. I find a good size for the
box is 2 feet long, 1½ feet wide, and 6″ deep. This will hold
about all the cement you'll want to mix up at one time for a
small repair job (40–45 pounds).

To mix the cement, dump it in the middle of the box, making
a small mountain. When the dust has cleared, take your pointing
trowel and make a hole about 8″ wide and as deep as possible in
the center of the mountain, turning it into a volcano. Fill the
hole with water and wait a few minutes. The powder and sand
will absorb a lot of the water, and then you're ready to mix the
stuff up. Once you've started mixing, keep adding water a little
at a time until the mix is loose enough to spread easily with the

trowel. Be careful with the water or you'll suddenly find the mix too soupy. It's amazing how quickly this can happen. You're mixing away, wondering when the stuff will ever be loose enough to work with, you add just a little too much water, and—mush. So take it easy. If it's soupy and runny, it won't have much strength.

Wet the bricks with an old paint brush and trowel the mortar over the wall just like plaster. If it doesn't stick too well and seems stiff, add a little more water. It takes experience to know when it's just the right consistency. Put the first layer on at least $\frac{1}{4}''$ thick. It doesn't have to be too smooth, but you don't want to leave big pieces of mortar sticking out because you'll find them hard to cover with the second coat.

Let the mortar harden for 20 minutes or so, then very lightly make lines in it with the edge of your trowel. This will give the next coat something to tie into.

The next day, wet the patch down lightly and apply the second coat, again at least $\frac{1}{4}''$ thick. In almost all cases, this will be enough to keep the inside of the wall safe from outside moisture. Some very damp spots may need three coats. You'll get better protection from three thin coats than from two thicker ones.

Under our Lawrence Street dining room window, the plaster was $1\frac{1}{2}''$ thick. I brought the mortar out to within about $\frac{1}{4}''$ of the surrounding wall, then finished off the repair with patching plaster. I had to use an awful lot of mortar to come out that far, and it was tough trying to get the finish plaster smooth over such a large area. The thought of plastering the rest of the dining room and the kitchen depressed me. But shortly after this, things began to look up: I discovered perlite plaster.

Perlite plaster is a base coat plaster made of volcanic rock. It is thick, light, easy to mix and apply and is excellent for filling large breaks in exterior walls. It adheres well to brick, plaster and concrete, to wood, metal, and gypsum lath. There are tiny air spaces in it, so it has some insulating value. It is sold in 40 or

80 pound bags, usually at masonry supply houses, often at lumber yards, and rarely at hardware stores, where it will cost a lot more. It goes by different brand names such as Structolite or Gypsolite.

I was first turned on to perlite plaster by Al Bonjourno, the man who fixed our chimneys on Lawrence Street. Al was a burly, baby-faced guy who wore a Stetson hat in even the hottest weather and constantly chewed on a cigar. He built a cement block flue for our heater and I watched as he covered it with a wonderful gooey gray material that went on with amazing ease. At the time I attributed the ease of application to Al's not inconsiderable skill as a plasterer, but I later found that I could do almost as well. The stuff fascinated me.

"Structolite," Al said, his giant biceps sweeping the trowel across the flue with impossibly competent strokes. "The great thing about it is you don't need no finish coat. You just throw a trowel full of cement in when you mix it, right? Then after you got it on, you let it set up and then you just wet your trowel and finish it off."

Wanting to know more, I went over and read the bag that the delicious-looking stuff had come in. It was a base coat for plaster, was not to be mixed with cement, and was to be used only over wood or gypsum lath, not masonry. While Al smoked and sweated, waiting for the plaster to set up, I timidly approached him. "Uh, I, uh, see here it says you're not supposed to use this over masonry."

Al's furry brows frowned under the hat. "Hah?"

"Like on brick and concrete you're supposed to use some other kind."

"What other kind?" Al said. "I ain't never seen no other kind."

"That's what it says on the bag," I said helplessly.

Al derisively sucked his cigar. "I never read what it says on them bags. Christ, we even use it outside on chimbleys."

"You can paint right over this?" I asked him later.

"Sure. Just wait a couple days till it dries out all the way. Yeah, we never mess with finish plaster no more."

The next day the stuff was hard as a rock. I decided to try it. I went to South Philly to the biggest masonry supply place I knew. "I'd like a bag of Structolite," I said to the rather harried looking man behind the counter. "—The kind you use on brick."

The guy wrote out a pink slip. "We only got one kind," he said. He didn't look at me, for which I was grateful.

"Oh," I said. "I thought there were two kinds. Can you use your kind on brick?"

He looked at me as he handed me the slip. "Sure can, sport." I didn't think the "sport" was called for.

I took the slip to the yard, hoping for the best. A giant and I wrestled the 80 pound sack into the back of my VW, and I read the label: it was the same stuff Al had used.

I gave it a try that afternoon. It worked out great. The patch I made with it held up perfectly for the six years we lived in that house. The stuff was much nicer than patching plaster in every way. Here's how you use it:

You'll need your mixing box (or an old plastic dishpan), plasterer's trowel, 3″ putty knife, and a bucket of water. Mix the stuff the same way you mix mortar: make a volcano and pour water down the hole. You'll find it much easier to mix than cement. Be careful you don't use too much water, but make it wet enough that it can be picked up easily on your trowel.

Soak the wall thoroughly. Smear the perlite onto it with your rectangular plasterer's trowel, building it up until the patch is flush with the existing plaster. You can put it on as thick as you want, but no thinner than about ¾ of an inch; it's too dense to use in thin coats. Unless you've made the mix really soupy, you shouldn't have any trouble with the stuff falling off the wall; its powers of adhesion are excellent.

Once the hole is filled, go over the patch lightly with the edge of your trowel and get it level with the existing wall and as smooth as possible. At this point you won't be able to get it completely smooth, so don't kill yourself. You'll notice that the surface has a lot of little holes in it. That's all right. You'll also notice that you've gotten perlite on the old plaster at the edge of the patch. Take the edge of the trowel (or your putty knife if it's easier) and scrape this excess off.

Let the perlite set up for about 20 minutes. It should feel just a bit less mushy than it did when you put it on. Now dip your trowel in a bucket of water and smooth it over the patch. The perlite won't shift around if it's set up enough, and you'll be able to smooth it off quite nicely. The smoothing process will close up almost all of the little holes. (There are always a few that resist; I hit them with vinyl spackle later.) Don't dip your trowel in the water so often that the perlite gets sopping wet, or you may end up with a powdery surface.

The edge of the patch is the hardest part to finish. You may have to wet it more than the rest to get it smooth, and your 3″ putty knife will usually do a better job than your trowel. If the edge of the patch does not blend satisfactorily into the wall when the perlite dries, go over it with some joint cement, which you can then rub and sand very smooth. If you're careful during the smoothing process, your perlite patch won't need any sanding at all.

Sometimes you'll find an area that needs a patch several inches thick. If you have some scraps of plasterboard around, you can save yourself some money and work by nailing them into the hole as a filler before you put on the perlite. If the wall is old brick, you can nail the plasterboard right into it, strange as this might seem. A smooth-shank blue nail will penetrate the old mortar between the bricks in most cases. Dick's helper George told me this, but I didn't believe him. He hammered a blue nail into a mortar joint on my kitchen wall and dared me to pull it out. I'm glad I didn't bet him money.

If you've had to cover the old brick with mortar, you won't be able to nail into it, so put a layer of perlite on, let it dry, then nail the plasterboard into that and finish with another coat of perlite.

Nail the plasterboard in with the finish side facing the brick, and cover the gray side with the perlite. The finish side of plasterboard is quite smooth; you'll find your perlite will slide around on it and it will be hard to get an even surface. It's also wise to scratch up the gray side with a nail or ice pick to give yourself an even rougher base.

What happened, you are asking, to the trowel full of mortar that Al said to throw into the perlite? I don't use it. I've found that you can get just as good results without it—and on two occasions when I used it, my perlite dried weak and powdery. Maybe this had nothing to do with the cement. Maybe I put too much water in the mix, or maybe the water was sucked out of the mix by an extremely thirsty brick wall. But I never had the problem when I left the mortar out, and leaving it out didn't seem to hurt, so why bother with it? Without adding anything to it, the perlite will set up like concrete. Actually, though, it is a good deal softer than concrete, and you'll be able to drive square-cut nails into it if you want to hang pictures later.

A word of caution: If your wall has been damaged by moisture, don't try to get away with skipping the mortar steps and just using the perlite alone. I've tried it. The moisture came through an inch and a half of the stuff, and I had to chip it all out and do the job over again.

You can fill holes in partitions with perlite, but unless they're small, don't bother. You'll find it easier to use plasterboard.

Furring Out—Is Out

If a wall is in very sad shape, with bulges, moisture damage, and old wallpaper, builders usually nail wood furring strips into it and cover them with new plasterboard. This is the cheapest way out for them, because scraping and chiseling and patching take time, time, time. Trouble is, they don't solve the moisture problems this way, and unless they've covered the furring with plastic sheets, someday the plasterboard may start to go. Since you're working on your old place in your spare time, it will be cheaper for you to scrape and chisel and patch (you don't have to do it all in one day, you know), and you'll be sure to foil the moisture.

Fixing a Hole in a Plasterboard Wall

Maybe your place has a plasterboard wall with a hole in it. Or maybe you've built a plasterboard-covered partition and have knocked a hole in it. A few good swings of a heavy door, and crash, the knob goes right through your wall. How do you fix it?

Holes in plaster walls are fairly easy to fix because there's a wood or metal lath on which to apply new plaster. But a hole in a plasterboard wall (or a plaster wall with gypsum lath) is pure gaping hole—there isn't any backing to put new plaster on, you have to provide one.

If the hole is really huge, you can cut the plasterboard back to the studs and nail in a whole new piece, the same way you'd fix a large break in plaster. But if the hole is small, you don't want to go to all that trouble.

What you do want to do is put a piece of something behind that hole and keep it there while you put on the patching plaster. I've run across various ways of doing this, and they all seem unnecessarily time-consuming and complicated. One method has you hammer four nails into the wall, run strings through the backing material (usually screen), and wrap the strings around the nails to hold the material in place. This means you make more holes in your wall, the nails will almost certainly come loose, and it will take a minor miracle to get the strings tight enough to keep the backing material flush with the hole.

When you do it my way, the first thing you need is a scrap of plasterboard. What if you haven't built a new partition or patched big holes in your walls and you don't have a piece of plasterboard lying around? Well, you might get away with using something else, like a couple of layers of corrugated cardboard.

But plasterboard is your best bet. Sometimes a lumberyard has plasterboard scraps that they'll either give you or sell you for next to nothing, and you can often find pieces in the trash at construction sites.

In addition to the plasterboard, you'll need the following: Plaster of Paris and patching plaster, a pan or dish to mix them in, a 1¼″ putty knife, a pointing trowel or 3″ putty knife, jar of water and old paint brush, utility knife, hammer and nail.

Take your utility knife and cut a scrap of plasterboard so that it's about 1″ narrower and 2″ longer than the hole you want to fix. Put the plasterboard on a board or a floor you don't care about and gently hammer the nail into the center of it. A blue nail is fine, or a 4d or 6d common nail. (Don't use a finishing nail, the head is too small.) Pick up the plasterboard and push on the head of the nail until it's snug against the plasterboard's surface.

Now mix up a small amount of Plaster of Paris with your putty knife. You want to use Plaster of Paris now for the very reason you don't want to use it for the other patching jobs I've described: its quick setting time. Don't make it too soupy and especially don't make it too stiff.

Next, make sure that the hole is free of crumbling plaster, dip your brush in the jar of water and wet the edges of the hole. Wet the face of the plasterboard too.

Now pick up the plasterboard, hold the shank of the nail with one hand (your left, if you're right handed) and insert the plasterboard into the wall so 1″ of it sticks up behind both the top and the bottom of the hole. (Remember, the plasterboard is *narrower* than the hole, so it will fit through it.) Now pull on the nail, bringing the plasterboard tight against the edges of the hole.

With your free hand, scoop up some Plaster of Paris on the small putty knife and press it into the edge of the hole. Repeat this process in four or five spots around the hole, continuing to pull on the nail with your other hand. Keep holding the nail for

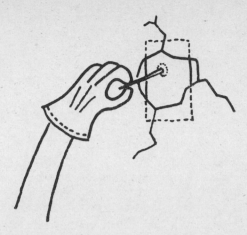

a couple of minutes, then gently let go. If your luck is rotten, the plasterboard will fall down inside the wall, but it's never happened to me yet. The Plaster of Paris should tack it in place, giving you a backing for your finishing material.

Wait about 15 minutes until the plaster is good and hard, then push on the shank of the nail (gently!) until it falls down inside the wall. Cover the plasterboard with patching plaster and smooth it off. And that's it.

So now you know how to keep your walls and ceilings from crashing down around you. We'll make them look pretty later on. Next, we'll talk about how you can make them keep you warm.

6 YOUR INSULATION

INSULATION IS STUFF YOU WRAP AROUND YOUR HOUSE TO KEEP the heat from leaving it too fast in winter—or to keep the heat from coming in when the weather's hot. It's also, secondarily, the stuff you can use to help give you peace and quiet. We'll get to that later.

You can insulate with all kinds of materials—sawdust, wood shavings, newspapers . . . But an ideal insulation has two important qualities that these particular materials lack: it will not absorb water readily and it will not burn.

In almost any discussion of insulation you will read that there are numerous types on the market: rock wool, cotton, fiberglass, and so on. But when you get right down to it, today fiberglass is king. You will have a tough time finding anything else. Most of what I'll have to say will be about fiberglass, though I'll also have something to say about foamed plastic.

You may see boats and shower stalls made of "fiberglass," but they are really a combination of fiberglass and plastic resins. Fiberglass itself is glass threads. It has a tendency to float through the air and irritate your skin and throat. "Pouring wool" (loose hunks of fiberglass) is especially good at this. Some brands of insulation are more wicked than others; some actually have glass slivers in them. The best I've used is Owens-Corning. But it's all irritating. Right after you work with fiberglass be sure to visit your mother so she can comment on the color in your cheeks. If you don't scratch and squirm in her presence, maybe she won't get suspicious.

Fiberglass won't burn. If you fill your walls with it, it acts as an effective fire stop. You may have also heard that its irritating particles repel vermin and rodents, but forget it. We stored some fiberglass insulation in our barn in Maine for a while, and one blanket I unrolled contained a nest of bumblebees. Another blanket squeaked. I tore it open and found five baby mice curled up as snug as can be. Maybe the pests will grow up emphysemic, but the fiberglass won't keep them out of your house.

Not so many years ago, insulation was an afterthought. In very old places, it wasn't even a thought. At worst, insulation was left to the wall materials themselves—brick, stone, or wood. At best it was left to a dead air space in the wall. As a matter of fact, this air space was far from "dead," since the warm inside surface and the cold outside surface set up convection currents. The problem was it provided only minimal protection.

In the exterior walls of frame houses there was a rather large air space, 4″ or so, and in some brick houses there was a space of maybe an inch, the thickness of the furring strip on which the lath was nailed. Actually, the 4″ space gave no more insulating value than the 1″ space. An air space ¾″ thick provides a very minimal amount of resistance to heat flow, about the same amount as ⅜″ of fiberglass. But you can make this air space as thick as you want beyond ¾″ and you won't improve its insulating value at all. So much for insulation in old houses. Not so great. Roof insulation was provided by snow.

Perhaps some of the disregard of insulation in the good old days was due to ignorance of its worth. There is still a lot of ignorance of its worth. The back room of our house on Lawrence Street was a brick addition exposed on two sides, with no room above it. We were having it furred out, and I wanted 3″ of fiberglass in the walls and 6″ in the ceiling. My contractor wanted 1½″ in the ceiling and none in the walls. "What do you want to waste your money for?" he argued. "Two courses of brick is as good insulation as you can get. Then on top of that you're gonna have furring strips and paneling, so you got a dead air space, too."

It is hard to come back with specifications from building manuals in the face of forceful arguments from burly contractors. At that point I didn't have any specs on hand to show the guy anyway, and he was all set to tackle the job. The materials he planned to use were already sitting in my house. (Did I ever regret having simply agreed to "insulation" in our talks, without having specified what kind of insulation and how much.)

The room was small, was to receive little use, and had a huge cast iron radiator, so I figured the man could have his way on the walls. But I put up a fight for the ceiling. "Listen," he said, "them companies just want you to buy their product. After the first inch and a half you gain so little by throwing in more that it ain't worth it. Anyway, you're gonna have a ceiling of pressed wood, and that'll give you all the extra insulation you'll need."

In a way there was some truth to what he said about insulation thickness and diminishing returns, as we'll see later. In no way was there any truth to the other things he said. He did the job his way. Do what I would, I never got the mammoth radiator to give off more than the bare minimum of heat. We froze. We had a nice room for storing apples.

"R" VALUES

To have a reasonably comfortable, efficient, and economical house, you should have at least 3½″ of fiberglass insulation in the walls, and at least 6″ in the ceiling.

Actually, "inches" is not a good way to talk about insulation.

You can take a fiberglass blanket nominally $3\frac{1}{2}''$ thick and fluff it up until it's $8''$ thick, or, conversely, squash it until it's about $1\frac{1}{2}''$ thick. What you really want to know is an insulation's "R" factor. "R" refers to a material's resistance to heat flow. In your walls, you want material with an R value of at least 11. In your ceilings you want at least R 19. Fiberglass blankets (long rolls) and batts (rectangular squares) have the R value printed on them. Other kinds of insulation often don't, and it may be hard to find out what their value is.

Some insulation is marked $4''$, some $6\frac{1}{2}''$, some will say "full thick" or something equally vague. You can forget all this nonsense as long as you know the R value, it's the only thing that counts.

Now, what can insulation do that walls alone can't? The typical, standard $3\frac{1}{2}''$ insulation has an R value of 11. How thick would a wood wall have to be to give this same degree of insulating value? Nine inches thick. Remember our cold storage locker on Lawrence Street. How thick would a *brick* wall have to be to insulate as well as R 11 fiberglass? Hang on, folks—4 *feet* thick. So you definitely want to insulate wherever you can, your wood or brick or plaster or air space just won't do the job. Insulation will not only save you fuel and money, it will make you a lot more comfortable as well.

I've said you'll want R 11 insulation in the walls and R 19 or better in the ceiling. Why heavier insulation in the ceiling? There is far more wall space in the house than ceiling space—but the rate of heat flow through the ceiling is much greater than the rate of heat flow through the walls, so you need that thicker stuff up there to slow down that rapid heat flow. Why not stick R 19 in the walls anyway just to be safe, since walls comprise such a large area? In the first place, R 19 insulation *is* around $6''$ thick, and unless your house is unusual, that's too thick to get into your walls—and when you compress insulation, you decrease its R value. In the second place, you now have to consider the diminishing returns I mentioned a minute ago.

According to *America's Handyman Book*, $1''$ of insulation

saves 12½ percent of your heat, 2″ saves another 3½ percent or a total of 16 percent, and 3″ saves a total of 17½ percent. This is a rather vague statement, to put it kindly, but you get the idea: for each added inch of insulation, you save proportionately less heat. Most authorities feel that adding more than 3″ in the walls and 6″ in the ceiling does not save enough fuel to justify the added expense of the insulating materials. Some authorities have upped these figures to 4″ and 9″, and add that after 9″ you can pile the stuff sky high and save a negligible amount of additional heat. So they say, at any rate. I'm not an engineer, but in general, I accept their basic principle.

VAPOR BARRIERS

As I've indicated, fiberglass insulation comes in several forms, in batts, blankets, and also in loose fill ("pouring wool"). Batts are rectangular blocks of the stuff, blankets are long rolls of the stuff and pouring wool is loose pieces of the stuff. Batts and blankets come with either an aluminum foil facing or a brown, asphalt-impregnated (kraft paper) facing. Batts also come with no facing.

The facing is important. It serves two purposes: it makes installation easier (we'll come to this), and it acts as a vapor barrier. A what? Here's where you can really get mixed up, so hang on.

We wash, we sweat, we boil water for our tea. Where does the "steam" go? It goes through the ceiling and walls. If it hits a spot that's cold enough, it condenses and turns to water. In the winter, if we have insulation in our walls, the inside of our exterior wall sheathing will be cold. Water vapor will condense on it the same as it will on a cold window pane. So what? Well, it gets your insulation wet, and when it's wet it doesn't insulate. In the old days there wasn't any insulation so you didn't have to worry too much about water vapor, though it could make the paint peel off your house. But when you insulate, you have to worry about it.

A vapor barrier is a layer of something that prevents the water vapor from going through the walls and condensing inside them. The vapor is never allowed to reach the "dew point"—it remains in your room as "humidity," something you usually can't get enough of in a heated house. Both kraft paper and foil are vapor barriers. Foil is supposed to be the better of the two, but kraft paper is perfectly okay.

We'll be very concerned with vapor barriers. The colder the climate, the more important they are.

WHERE TO INSULATE

What do you insulate? Anything that has cold air on the other side of it: The upstairs ceiling, the outside walls, the wall that adjoins the garage, the floor over a crawl space. The various manufacturers of insulation have brochures that show you just what parts of a house to insulate, and there are sections in most handyman books discussing this, so I won't go into it further here. I want to discuss some of the things these books and brochures either don't tell you or don't go into detail about.

INSULATING THE WALLS

Since heat flow is greater through the roof than it is through the walls, you'll want to insulate your ceiling even if you insulate nothing else. An attic ceiling is the easiest spot to insulate in an old place—so we'll discuss it later and get right into the hard part, the walls.

There are three main ways to insulate an existing wall: put something inside it, cover it with something, or tear it down to the studs and insulate as you would in new construction. For the sake of illustration, let's insulate a brand new wall. This is to provide some contrast with what *you* will run into, and send you into a fit of gloom.

Batt and blanket insulation is made in 15″ and 23″ widths. These widths are designed to fit between the conventional 16″ and 24″ on center spacing of the studs and rafters in most of today's construction. (But your old house was built in a different era, the era of, from what I can deduce, "Hey, how about we put a stud here? Look good to you?" Either that, or everyone in the building trades was drunk. Your old place doesn't have its studs 16″ on center. You're lucky if it has its studs *anything* on center.) But our wall here, our brand new wall, does have its studs 16″ on center, and here's how we insulate it.

The Ideal Situation

These are the materials you'll need: 15″ R 11 blanket insulation, butcher knife or large shears, yardstick (metal preferred), staple gun.

Why blanket insulation? It comes in long rolls, and so it has fewer seams than batts. Every seam means another possible vapor leak. And you will also probably not be able to get R 11 insulation in anything *but* blankets.

Before you put the blankets in, all wiring and plumbing must be completed. You tuck insulation between the wall sheathing and any pipes to keep them from freezing.

Cut each piece of insulation about 8″ longer than the height of the room. This will give you 4″ at both the floor and the ceiling to squash in tight against the plates so you don't get any drafts. How do you cut the insulation? If you have a big butcher knife, and I do mean a big one, sharpen it up, put the insulation on a scrap of hardboard or particle board or something else you don't care about, and cut it using a sawing motion or several long, straight strokes. It's best to turn it paper side down. You can compress the "wool" with a metal straight edge, but it isn't really necessary. Once you're through the wool you may find it easier to cut the paper or foil with scissors rather than the knife. (You can cut insulation paper-side up, but you're more likely to tear the paper that way. If you cut it paper-side up, it's better to use the shears.)

Remember: the warm, moist air flows from inside the house through the walls and ceiling to the outdoors. So you always install insulation with the vapor barrier facing the heated living space. So with the paper or foil side facing you, press the blanket in place between the studs until the fiberglass touches the wall sheathing. Don't compress it, but make sure it touches the sheathing; you don't want air circulating between the sheathing and the insulation. There are paper flanges about 1" wide on both sides of the blanket. Staple them with your staple gun to

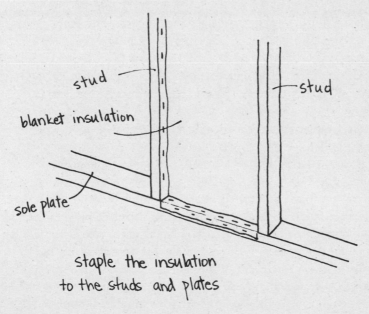

staple the insulation
to the studs and plates

the inside surface of the studs. Use staples at least ⁵⁄₁₆″ long. Put one in every 6 to 8 inches. At the top and bottom of the blanket, pull away a few inches of paper from the wool, cram the wool tightly against both the sole plate and the top plate, then staple the paper to the plates.

You're looking at the blanket and saying, hey, I put those staples every 6 to 8 inches, but there are still little gaps between the flanges and the studs. You're right, there are little gaps. Obviously, water vapor is going to pass through those gaps. The insulation companies keep their mouths shut about this. You'll also have gaps where you've cut holes for your electrical boxes. What's more—you might as well know the worst—you'll have rips in your barrier. I don't care how careful you are, you are going to rip that paper or foil, it's impossible not to.

What can you do? For the rips, you can use a plastic tape like Mystic tape, but in some spots it might not stick. The gaps? If your barrier is paper, you can staple your flanges to the *face* of the studs instead of to the sides. But you don't want to do this if it will keep your fiberglass from touching the sheathing. (You also don't want to do this if your barrier is foil; you'll see why in a minute.)

Some kinds of insulation have a 2″ flange instead of a 1″ flange. With this stuff, you can staple one inch to the inside of the stud, fold the other inch over the face of the stud and staple it there. But watch out—sometimes this paper is not a vapor barrier, and following this procedure won't do you any good. (It's a vapor barrier if it's thick and has black strands of asphalt through it.)

Okay, the best method to follow in order to insure a really tight vapor barrier is to staple overlapping sheets of polyethylene plastic over the entire wall after you've installed your fiberglass. This stuff is not expensive, and if you get the 4 mil thickness, it's easy to handle. The building supply carries it. It usually comes in sheets 3, 4, and 6 feet wide. (You may find it in sheets 8 feet wide or wider, but in these large sizes it's tough to manipulate.)

Run the sheets across the wall horizontally and overlap them about a foot. (For an 8 foot high wall, for example, buy a roll 6 feet wide and a roll 3 feet wide.) Stretch it so it's not slack, and just go right over any electrical boxes. Later, take a knife and cut an "X" in the plastic in the middle of each box, and stretch the plastic around the box's edge. This gives you a really tight fit around the box. Instead of plastic you could use kraft paper sheets or builder's foil (not the supermarket kind), but you'd probably tear that too.

You don't need the extra plastic barrier in all climates, but if the winter temperature regularly drops below 25 degrees, it's good to have it.

A vapor barrier will never be perfectly tight, and you're bound to punch some small holes in it when you nail up your plasterboard or hang a picture, but as long as there aren't any major rips, you're okay.

If you use foil-faced insulation, which is more expensive than kraft-faced, you will probably find instructions that say to be sure to leave at least $3/4''$ of air space between the foil and the inside wall covering—the plasterboard or whatever. If you have stapled the flanges to the inside of the studs you will automatically have this. Why is it important? Because foil itself is an insulator, but to be effective, it must have an air space of at *least* $3/4''$ in front of it. If you apply it properly, you get insulating value over and above the R rating for the fiberglass alone. Provided you have a $3/4''$ air space, a foil facing on R 11 fiberglass increases the resistance to R 13. If, however, the foil touches the plasterboard, its insulating value is largely lost. (Don't bother to use foil-faced insulation on ceilings, because gravity will make it impossible for you to maintain the $3/4''$ air space.)

Another question arises: What about the studs themselves? Doesn't a lot of heat escape through them? Well, if it takes $9''$ of wood to equal $3\frac{1}{2}''$ of fiberglass in insulating value, the answer is obviously yes. But there's nothing you can do about it.

We have just finished insulating the ideal wall. Unless you've built one, you won't find an ideal wall in your old place. So how do you proceed? Let's talk about frame houses first.

Frame Houses and Blown Insulation

The most practical way to insulate an existing wall in a frame house is not a way that you can do yourself: you have an insulation contractor blow fiberglass into the spaces between your studs. To do this he has to cut holes in the outside of your house and stick a hose in your walls. (He'll repair the holes.)

A do-it-yourself way to achieve roughly—sometimes pretty roughly—the same result is to get up in the attic and pour vermiculite down between your studs. (I am assuming, for the moment, that these spaces between the studs are accessible from up there.) Vermiculite is small, light granules of mica sold in building supply houses under various brand names such as Zonolite. You pour it between each stud space until you can't pour any more. Theoretically, when this happens, you've filled the space from the ground up to the roof. Chances are you haven't. You may have filled it from the second floor up, though. The R value of any of this is anyone's guess, but at least it's better than plain air.

The problem with both the blown-in wool and the vermiculite is twofold: How do you know if the stuff really filled all the spaces in your walls unless you take a giant X-ray of your house? And what about a vapor barrier? Webster's says vermiculite is ". . . a lightweight highly water-absorbent material." Doesn't sound too good.

Any paint on the walls inside your rooms, however, acts as a vapor barrier. Some paints are better barriers than others. None is as good as plastic, foil, or kraft paper. The best thing, according to what I've read, is two coats of aluminum paint under your finish paint. Working with aluminum paint is far from my idea of a good time, but if you gotta . . . It also has a tendency to show up gray through some finish coats, so if you use it, seal it with shellac or a shellac-based primer (see the section on painting). An oil-based primer and two coats of latex-based paint is also supposed to be an effective vapor barrier. This doesn't sound like too bad a proposition.

There is no other "easy" solution to the vapor barrier problem in old houses. If your walls didn't bulge too much but needed a new surface, you could cover them with foil-backed plasterboard (if you could get it), nailing it right over the existing wall. You could fur your wall out with 1″ wood strips nailed through the plaster and into the old studs, then staple polyethelene over this and cover it all with new plasterboard. But with either of these methods you are going to have to move all of the switch and outlet boxes forward—not an easy or pleasant job—and you will also have to work out some solution for your windows and doors, taking off the moldings and replacing them and compensating for the added wall thickness. All this is a terrible amount of money, time, and trouble.

Item: If your exterior walls are made of solid planks, you're basically just out of luck—but see p. 104.

Using Blankets in Old Walls

If your plaster is in rotten shape and you're going to remove it, you'll be able to insulate your walls with blankets as we did our ideal wall. Well, not exactly—because your studs, you remember, will be spaced at random. So you'll probably need both 15″ and 23″ blankets to fit the variety of widths you'll encounter.

Sometimes you'll have more than 23″ between the studs, and you'll have to run the insulation the long way across them in order to span the distance. Be sure to cut the pieces of blanket long enough to give a good snug fit, and butt the edges of each piece tightly against the next one.

Save all scrap for stuffing around windows, doors, electrical boxes, behind pipes, any place there's a hole. If you go over the wall with plastic, you don't have to worry if you have spots where there's no foil or paper.

Brick Houses

What if you have a brick house? In brick row houses, remember that you insulate only the walls exposed to the cold, never a party wall—unless you think the house next door will be torn down. The other side of your party wall is warm from your neighbor's heater. If you don't have a corner house, you get warmed on both sides. You *do* want to insulate those exterior walls. However . . .

If the walls are furred out so there's an air space, you can try the vermiculite again. But if your plaster's been applied right over your brick, you're out of luck. As you are in frame houses where the exterior walls are made of solid planks—although the wood will give you more insulating value than the masonry.

If you're determined to insulate your walls in places like these, the most practical thing to do is to build a new stud wall in front of your existing wall and insulate that. Since you're simply building a frame to support insulation and plasterboard, you can use 2 x 3s spaced 24″ on center. Secure this frame to the floor and ceiling as you would an interior partition. Some contractors use this method in renovating frame houses too, instead of tearing out the old plaster walls. It eats up floor space, but it saves the dirty work of tearing out, and chances are if you do tear out, the old studs will be so uneven and out of plumb that you'll end up building a new wall anyway.

You could also fur out the walls and place sheets of either polystyrene ("styrofoam") or urethane insulating board between the furring strips, then cover with new plasterboard. You nail the furring strips into the old plaster with square-cut nails and a heavy hammer, or put them up with a special adhesive. (The building supply can tell you what adhesive to use.) This method saves space, but you'll have trouble getting the furring strips up if your walls are bulged or if the plaster is in bad shape.

Either of these methods gives you the problem with the outlet boxes and doors and windows. So in old brick houses like these, I'd be content to do a good job in the attic.

ATTIC CRAWL SPACES

The two most practical ways to reduce heat loss in an old house are to insulate the attic and install storm windows. You lose about 25 percent of your heat through the ceiling and about 12 percent through your windows, so these two measures can save you a lot. I'll get to the windows later. Let's do the ceiling.

Old houses that haven't been fooled around with have an attic or crawl space. If there's a crawl space, there's a good chance that the joists inside it have not been covered with boards. If this is the case, you're in luck, relatively speaking. I mean relatively speaking because insulating a crawl space is not a whole lot of fun no matter how you go about it.

My initiation into insulation was a crawl space job, and no perverse fraternity could've devised a more fiendish torture than the one I inflicted upon myself.

Our bathroom on Lawrence Street was a converted bedroom, twelve-by-fifteen feet, with fireplace. In those days we thought it romantic to have a huge bathroom, and because we thought it so, it was. It was also cold. Very cold. Two and a half of its brick walls faced the frigid air, and there was no other room above it. We had a cast iron baseboard radiator that heated up okay, but on really cold days did little more than keep the pipes from freezing.

The roof over this bathroom was a shed-type extending about four feet above the ceiling at its highest point. After suffering through our first winter, I decided that as soon as the weather turned warm I would insulate that bathroom ceiling crawl space.

On a pleasantly warm day in May, I crawled through a hole in the ceiling, shoving my bags of fiberglass "pouring wool" ahead of me. Pouring wool is a lot cheaper than batts (it's hunks of batts and blankets that they screwed up on at the factory), and since it's loose pieces, you can shove it into all sorts of out of the way corners. It's the perfect thing for old crawl spaces. Just perfect.

I don't think I've ever spent a more miserable day in my life outside of the hospital. The pleasantly warm day in the bathroom was a most unpleasant inferno in the crawl space. I couldn't *believe* the heat. Above my head was an asphalt-covered metal roof, and there was no ventilation whatsoever. The 100 watt bulb I'd hung in the blackness burned like a malevolent sun, setting my cheeks ablaze. I was scrunched on the joists in a disc-wrenching squat, fearful of a major slip that would send my knee or shoe smashing through the plaster ceiling below me.

But the best was yet to come. I tore open one of the bags of insulation, grabbed a huge handful of the stuff, and stuck it between the joists. Immediately my sun was orbited by a billion sparkling planets, which I, needing oxygen desperately, began to inhale. Dripping with sweat, coughing, throat and skin beginning to prickle madly, I fled from this calamity to fetch my dust mask.

I guess the mask did some good, but most of the time it smothered me and set me to gulping glass dust through my mouth. Many times did I descend into the land of the cool, the land of light and air, before my task was done.

I used up all the wool and then I took my ruler as they tell you to and measured the depth of the insulation. Well, it was 3″ here, 6″ there, 8″ over in the corner. I spread the wool out as evenly as I could. Now it was 4″ everywhere—but in some places the 4″ was all fluffed up, in others the stuff was squashed together. Was 4″ of fluff equal to 4″ of squash? Couldn't be. How would I ever be able to tell when I'd insulated evenly? I threw my ruler into the land of light, disgusted.

It was warmer in the bathroom the next winter, but it was a warmer winter. I really don't know how effective my insulation was. In the first place, I had no ventilation in that space. In the second place, I had no vapor barrier. These two errors combined—above a bathroom, where showers and such go on— probably guaranteed wet, useless insulation all winter long.

Any attic crawl space should be ventilated. You should install louvered vents in the walls at each end of the space. (There are also roof vents available if you can't manage this.) Provide at least 1 square foot of ventilation for every 300 square feet of crawl space floor area. If you increase this to 1 square foot per 150 square feet of floor area, you don't need a vapor barrier across your ceiling insulation: the circulating air alone will take care of any moisture. This ventilation will also reduce heat build-up in the summer tremendously.

The other mistake in my crawl space job, of course, was that I didn't insulate heavily enough. I should've had at least 6″ of stuff in that space. I still don't know how you tell when you have 6″ of insulation—or, more precisely, R 19—when you use pouring wool. Because of this, and because of its vicious nature, I haven't used it since.

If I had it to do over, I'd use 6″ batt insulation. This comes in pieces approximately 2 x 4 feet, and it doesn't fly all over the place. It has an R 19 value, so you know where you stand. You can cut it to fit odd spaces easily enough. If you need a vapor barrier, you can lay poly plastic over the crawl space floor before you put the insulation down, stapling the plastic against the floor joists where they meet the lath and plaster, or you can paint the ceiling of the room below with two coats of aluminum paint. For a fast, unirritating insulation job you could use vermiculite. But 2″ of vermiculite equals 1″ of fiberglass. So for an R 19 rating, you'd have to put 12″ of the stuff between the joists. Good luck. In crawl spaces too shallow to work in, you can have fiberglass blown in.

ATTICS

While a crawl space is likely to have joists exposed, an attic is likely to have them covered with floorboards. In order to insulate, you have to pry up enough of these boards to let you shove your material into all the spaces. Some fun.

But if you are going to use the attic as living space, then you can insulate the underside of the roof instead of the attic floor. If the rafters are exposed, this is a job you can do yourself. You'll probably run into odd spacing again. Insulate with faced batts, the same way you would a wall. Run them horizontally in the spaces wider than 23″, and cover them with plastic to assure a tight vapor barrier. But *don't* push the fiberglass right up against the sheathing as you would in a wall. You're supposed to allow about an inch of air space between the roof sheathing and the insulation for ventilation purposes.

If your rafters are covered with lath and plaster, as they were in our Lawrence Street house, you're faced with a more formidable problem. Actually, although we never did it, we could've insulated that attic fairly simply. There was a small crawl space above the attic ceiling. We could've filled the floor of this with batts, and while we were up there, poured vermiculite down behind the plaster that covered the slanted parts of the ceiling. If there are holes in your eaves, though, watch it—the vermiculite will pour right out into the air. In cases where there are such holes, you can shove batts down into the ceiling with a stick. This is a tricky, time-consuming, dusty job. Don't use faced material in this kind of installation, you'll tear the foil or paper to shreds. If you can't get anything into the space yourself, have it blown in.

OPEN BEAMS

Suppose you want to leave the beams exposed in the ceiling of your top floor. How do you insulate between them?

If the beams are deep enough, you can of course nail furring strips to their sides and staple batts or blankets to the strips, then cover them with plasterboard. The beams probably won't be deep enough. In this case, the best solution is to fit sheets of urethane foam between them. Two inches of urethane has an R value of 13, equal to 3½" of fiberglass with a properly installed foil vapor barrier. Three inches of urethane is R 19.5, equal to 6" of fiberglass. Styrofoam is usually easier to find than urethane, but it has a lower R value (2" equals R 8). You don't need a vapor barrier with these materials. Also, they are expensive compared to fiberglass.

If you use them, hold the sheets in place with wood strips, and nail plasterboard over the material into these strips. Most of this plastic stuff burns like mad, and uncovered it is very dangerous.

CELLAR CRAWL SPACES

Your old house will probably not have a cellar running its entire length; there may be a section at the back of the place where you have a crawl space. The floor above this crawl space should be insulated, because it's *cold* underneath those boards. Plan to get under there in the summer, when it's warm.

A natural mistake in this type of installation is to put the fiberglass in with the vapor barrier facing the ground—natural because it looks like the only way you *can* put it in. But remember, the barrier should face the *heated* space, the underside of the floorboards in this case. You need a special kind of insulation for this called "reverse flange," which will let you staple the barrier in place the right way. But your joists will probably not be 16″ or 24″ on center anyway, and you'll have to staple plastic sheeting to the underside of your floorboards, then stick in fiberglass batts and hold them in place by stapling chicken wire across the bottom of your joists. You do all this while lying on your back, of course. Now you know why most people (including myself) have uninsulated crawl spaces.

Actually, out of all the people I've known who have old houses, only one had a cellar crawl space accessible enough to insulate. The others (including myself) had spaces too shallow to get into. Now of course if you're taking up the old floor, your joists will be exposed and you can insulate just as you would a wall. But . . . if you don't put chicken wire across the bottom of the joists, pretty soon the fiberglass will fall away from the foil or kraft paper. If you're laying a new floor over the old one, you can put insulation board down before you lay your new floorboards. This will help a little. If you're not doing either of these things and you can't get into the crawl space, you're out of luck. About the best you can do is what they do in Maine: stick bales of hay around your house to block off that cold wind.

Stuffing your place with insulation isn't all you can do to beat the cold. Storm windows and weatherstripping will help a lot, and we'll get to them in the next chapter.

INSULATION FOR QUIET

Shortly after we were married we were having a talk at the table in our tiny kitchen, going on into the night about this and that, when a voice like a foghorn rang out loud and strong, "Knock it off in there, willya, I'm trying to get some sleep." Silently we folded our cake and crept into the living room. Our kitchen and the bedroom of the apartment next door were apparently separated by little more than a pair of electrical boxes and two outlet plates, one on our side and one on theirs. This discovery crimped our spontaneity, though since it was their bedroom but only our kitchen, it undoubtedly crimped theirs more than it did ours.

The partitions of today, a string of studs and a couple of sheets of plasterboard, don't do much to hold sound down. If you're building partitions like this in your place, unless you like to hear the kids' records while you're reading, or the washer while you're taking a nap, you ought to do something to muffle things.

The best sound insulation is a closet full of clothes. The second-floor plan of our house in Maine looks like this:

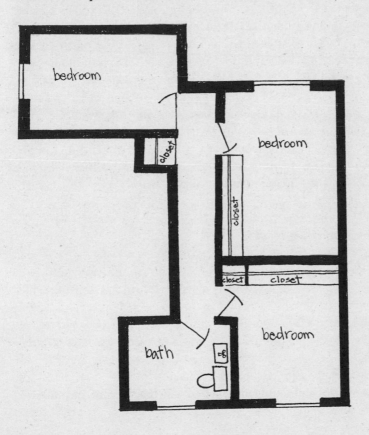

This wasn't strictly accidental. The closets provide a good sound barrier between hall and bedroom and between bedroom and bedroom. But there are times when you can't work things out this way and you have to do something to the wall itself.

People have been wrestling with this problem for some time. Proust lined his study with cork. Now if Proust himself were very noisy and he had fussy neighbors, this wall treatment would've been fine. Cork-lined walls will quite effectively cut down on sounds originating in a room and provide a nice, dead quality that people like Proust probably like. However you may not care for the sound of the noises in your ears after a while, and the cork will do little or nothing to keep sound *out* of your room—unless, of course, all the walls in the house are lined with cork, or celotex, or tapestries, or egg cartons, or acoustic tiles so that they're all dead and none can transmit much of anything to any other room. If you like that idea, you're all set.

If you like a more lively sound in your rooms, and if you want the smooth surface of plasterboard to paint in a manner of your choosing, you will want to do something *inside* your wall to block sound passage from room to room.

Building a wall with excellent noise control qualities is a tricky job. You can, however, create a wall with *good* noise control fairly simply.

Staggered Stud Wall

The most common noise control wall shown in handyman books is the staggered stud wall. I've never built one myself, so here I am mostly reporting what others say to do. If you build this type of wall out of 2 x 4 studs, you use 2 x 6s for your sole and top plates instead of the usual 2 x 4s. You erect one wall of studs along one edge of the plates, and, between these, another row along the opposite edge of the plates.

Thus the studs and plasterboard on one side of the wall are

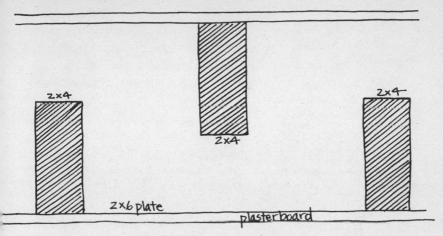

the staggered stud wall

separate from the studs and plasterboard on the other side of the wall. This cuts down on sound transmission dramatically.

Noise can be further reduced by installing 3½″ fiberglass blanket insulation, either weaving it between the studs or stapling it between the studs on one side of the wall. Either way works equally well, according to the laboratory results I've seen.

This wall takes up two more inches of floor space than a standard 2 x 4 partition. An alternative is to build the wall with 2 x 3 studs on 2 x 4 plates. This would take up no more room than a standard partition and would deaden noise almost as effectively as the thicker staggered stud wall. It just wouldn't feel as solid.

There are some difficulties with this kind of wall. Staggered stud construction uses twice as many studs as a standard wall, which means a lot of work. And if you're not going to build it yourself, just try to find a carpenter who'll build it for you.

There are unanswered questions in the construction of these partitions, too. The drawings in the books I've read are always like the one on p. 113—they show you a section in the middle of the wall. But how are the studs set up at the end of the wall? And what happens at a doorway? How do you provide support for the ends of your plasterboard without having the studs touch? I guess in a wall with 2 x 6 plates and 2 x 4 studs, you turn one 2 x 4 like this:

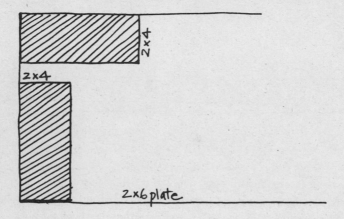

This will still give you ½" of air space between them. But what if you want to save space and build the wall out of 2 x 3s? How do you handle the doorways and ends? It seems you'd have to turn *both* sideways, like this:

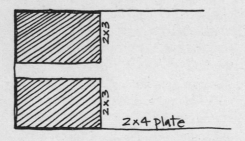

This solution also keeps the studs apart by ½".

Slit-Stud Wall

Now, you can also build the whole wall this way, with all the 2 x 3s turned sideways, but right opposite each other instead of staggered. This is called the "slit-stud" method, and is supposed to do almost as good a job at cutting down on noise as the staggered stud method. You'll have to build it on 16" centers if you want something sturdy.

Insulation Board Wall

A much easier noise control partition for the handyman to build is the following: Construct a standard stud framing and over the studs nail sheets of ½" sound insulating (or "deadening") board. Over this, glue ½" plasterboard, using wallboard and paneling adhesive. This gives you almost as much sound control as the staggered stud wall, takes up only an extra inch of floor space, and saves you the trouble of cutting and installing those extra studs. It brings the surface of your wall out farther on each side, though, so if you plan to build this way, remember to set your electrical boxes out the extra ½". This is the ideal noise-control wall for the amateur builder. Less sawing than staggered or slit studs, and no trouble at doorways or ends of partitions.

There's only one catch: you may not be able to find sound deadening board. A lot of places say they carry it, but all they have is celotex. If you can't get it, what do you do? You can do something, but not too much.

First, you can staple 3½" kraft-paper–covered fiberglass blankets between your studs. This is better than nothing, but not a whole lot. After you do this, you could cover one side of the wall with celotex before you put on your plasterboard. This would help a little more.

Styrofoam

On Lambert Street, Dick sound-insulated a standard partition by tightly fitting 2″ thick styrofoam board between the studs. The books never mention this, and from what I've read, theoretically it shouldn't be too effective. But it worked out fine for us. The stuff not only blocked airborne sound, but, because of its tight fit, cut down on stud vibration as well, and we were really pleased with the results. (Our bedroom was on one side of the wall, a cantankerous ten-year-old clothes dryer was on the other side.)

Sound Absorbers in Partitions

Acoustic fiberglass panels, the kind in the ubiquitous suspended ceiling, are tremendous at soaking up sound within a room. Will they work inside your walls? To a certain extent, they will (I've tried them). But they're almost twice as expensive as blanket insulation, and according to what I've read, they aren't any better. Apparently, sound absorbing materials such as these (and foamed plastic and Proust's cork) are much less effective inside a wall than they are on its surface. But I knew someone who glued egg cartons inside his partition with excellent sound-deadening results, so it's hard to say.

You might want to cover your ceiling with one of these sound-absorptive materials even if you don't want one on your walls. Our hallway on Lambert Street was much quieter once we put up our styrofoam cups, and it soaked up sound that would've otherwise found its way into the study and bedrooms.

HOLES

If you have old plaster partitions in your house, you will probably have no problem with sound transmission. With a thick layer of plaster and a layer of wood lath on each side of the studs, you're in good shape. But you can screw things up by putting new electrical outlets back to back in a wall like this. This is what happened with the wall in our first apartment. When the place was rewired, the electrician made things easy for himself and installed the outlets back to back, creating a hole in a solid wall that would ordinarily have let little sound pass through.

Some sound will come through any openings in a wall, so it's a good idea to caulk around electrical boxes and to caulk the joint between the floor and the plasterboard in a new partition before you install the baseboard. There are acoustical caulks designed for this purpose.

EXPOSED BRICKS

If you plan to expose the bricks on a party wall, remember: That thick old plaster helps cut out noise, and once it's off, your neighbors will sound louder.

7 YOUR WINDOWS AND DOORS

DOORS AND WINDOWS TAKE A LOT OF PUNISHMENT: THEY'RE constantly being slammed in and out or up and down, constantly being battered by wind, rain, sun, and snow. The doors and windows in your old place will probably need lots of work; they certainly have in our old places. You'll find doors that don't close, that are coming apart at the seams, that hang from loose hinges, and windows that are rotten, painted shut, broken or missing completely.

RENOVATING OLD WINDOWS

Windows have a lot of seams and corners and angles; if they aren't cared for on a regular basis, they fall apart. Actually, it's amazing how well windows stay together after years and years of neglect, and how when they look just awful they can often be made to function again.

118

Most old places will have double hung windows—the common windows with upper and lower sash (the parts of the window that contain glass) that slide up and down—and most of these windows will be made of wood. Some not-so-old places may have casement windows made of metal. These can get rusted and bent and forget how to close properly; they will need paint and oil and perhaps weatherstripping, but they should hold up pretty well. The double hung sash can fall apart completely.

New windows cost a lot of money, and wherever you can, it's worth it to repair the old ones. However, where all the corners of the sash are loose, half the panes are missing, the putty has crumbled away and the muntins (the little cross pieces of wood that hold the panes) are rotten, forget it. It's true that even sash in this sad condition can be renewed, I've done it. But it isn't worth it; buy new ones.

In some old places, though, you will run into sash that you can't replace today—unless you have them made at a mill, which will usually cost a small fortune. On Lambert Street the large windows on the front of our house had curved tops. You do not go down to your friendly lumberyard and pick up that kind of number nowadays. We had no choice but to fix the old windows.

Taking the Window Apart

To work on old sash, you have to take them out of the window frame. This is done, fortunately, from inside the house. There are strips of wood around the inside of the frame, "sash peak," that hold the bottom sash in place. Pry them off with a pry bar or old screwdriver and try not to break them. Sash peak is expensive, and you may not be able to match the kind your house has. Once the sash peak is off, you can take the lower sash out.

In rare cases, this lower sash will still be in working order. If

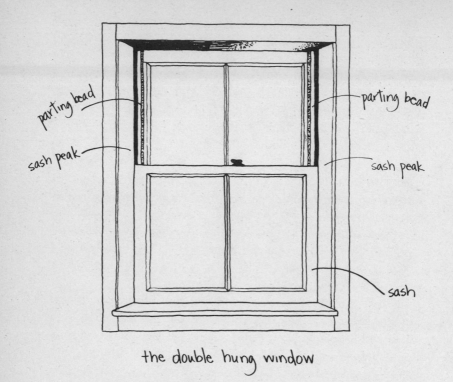

parting bead

parting bead

sash peak

sash peak

sash

the double hung window

so, you will see cords or chains attached to its sides. These run up to the top of the frame and disappear over little wheels. You have to take these cords off the sash in order to remove it. They are attached to weights inside the window frame, and before you remove them, if they aren't knotted, stick a nail through one of the chain links or tightly tape a little piece of wood to the cord—or else, once the thing is free of the sash, zip, it's out of your hand and over the wheel and gone so fast you won't believe it. Put a mark on both the sash and the cord at the spot where the cord's attached. Then you'll know just where to reattach it later on.

The lower sash is out. There are thin wood strips, "parting beads," holding the upper sash in place. These are set in grooves in the frame, and it takes some doing to pry them out without breaking them. If they're rotten at the bottom (and they usually are), resign yourself to buying new ones. They are a standard item at the lumberyard. The upper sash may be painted in place. If hammer taps and chisel scrapes won't loosen it, you'll have to soften the paint with your propane torch.

Fixing the Sash

You have both sash out. Put them on a table or workbench and check them over again carefully. If a couple of the corners are a bit chewed, some of the putty is missing, and the paint is gone but the wood is basically sound, it's worth it to renovate.

Scrape off all the loose paint and putty. You can get the putty out with a pocket knife. If there's a broken pane you want to replace, you'll have to get all its putty out, and this will take some softening with a soldering iron or propane torch. Scrape any paint off the sides of the sash, the part where the cord attaches. Sand these sides lightly. Don't repaint them. Paint on these surfaces will interfere with the operation of the window. Once the front of the sash (the part that faces the outdoors) is clean, real clean, paint it with an exterior primer. Be sure to paint the inside part of the muntins where the new glass will go. This will keep the old wood from drawing oil or water out of the new putty (I'll call it putty, but you'll be using something else, as we will discuss shortly) and help it to stick better. Let the primer dry thoroughly.

Next, reinforce the bad corners. You can do this several ways: By drilling holes through the corners and tapping glue-soaked dowels into them (use waterproof glue); by using metal corner braces screwed onto the outside face of the corner. (Don't put the braces in with nails, they won't hold tightly. And make sure to set the braces in far enough from the edge of the sash so they won't hit the frame or parting bead when you install the sash again.)

Davene's father did a terrific job on the corners of our Lambert Street windows with his glue gun. A glue gun is inexpensive and for this kind of job it's great. If you can pull the corner joints apart a little, shove glue into them as deeply as you can, push the corners back together, then spread some glue over the outside of the joints. If any of the muntins seem weak, hit them with the glue gun too.

Replacing Glass

Next replace broken glass. Glass is not terribly cheap either, and if you have some around you might want to try to cut it to fit the sash. I am not going to talk about this job here, most handyman books have very good descriptions of it. It's a job I hate. Wear goggles, and by all means buy one of the carbide-tipped cutters, they really do work better. Wear leather gloves.

It is more expensive but much less frustrating and dangerous to buy a new piece of glass and have it cut for you. You can usually buy glass at your hardware store, lumberyard, or paint store, and there are places that deal in nothing but glass. All of these places either have fantastic giant glass cutters or whole machines that do the job in a flash. You have already removed the old glass and putty. Now, measure the exact size of the opening in the sash, then deduct ⅛″ from each dimension. When you get the glass cut, be sure to tell the man that these are the exact dimensions of the piece of glass you want. Otherwise he is likely to assume you have given him the size of the opening and haven't taken any leeway into consideration, and he'll deduct *another* ⅛″.

In Philadelphia I used to get my glass at a giant glass place run by a glowering, sour guy who always wore an overcoat. I'd be sour too if I had to cut glass all day, but in July I'd do without the coat. He would crunch around in the sparkling shreds and snap at me like a Pekinese, all the time cutting with his huge red cutter and his motion smooth as silk. Once I had the nerve to give him a dimension like, "Twenty-five and three-sixteenth inches wide." "What?" he snarled. "What do you want, a glove fit for Chrissake?" And he cut the glass ⅛″ shorter, the pane was too small, and I had to make up the difference with putty.

Glazing Compounds

Though I used putty, the books say you should use glazing compound, very much like putty and applied the same way. It's pretty good, I've used it a number of times. I've also used white lead putty, very nice to work with and fine for destroying the brains of small children, so be careful. I have also used—here's heresy—caulking compound.

Before you put your pane of glass in, smear a little of your "putty," whatever it may be, around the inside of the muntin, then lay the glass in place on top of this. Hold it there with glazier's points, two if you have a small pane, more for larger panes. Get "push points," not the old fashioned triangular kind. Push points are easy to push into place with a screwdriver and it won't slip off them while you're doing it.

Next apply your glazing material. If it's putty or glazing compound, you roll a wad of it between your fingers, forming a snakelike strand. Press the strand firmly into place around the edge of the pane. Then pull your putty knife along the putty at an angle, smoothing it off. The knife will do a better smoothing job if it's dipped in a little paint thinner (if you're using an oil-base compound) or water (if you're using latex base).

If you use caulking compound, just squirt it right on from the gun as you would in any other application. It won't give you quite as smooth a bead as putty, but once you get the hang of it you'll be able to get it smooth enough. It is just as permanent as glazing compound if not more so, and it goes on much faster and with much less trouble. My father used it on his windows over thirty years ago and they have held up fine so far. Don't use the most expensive caulk for this, (butyl rubber, for example), use the standard grade.

One surprise if you've never used a caulking gun before: when you're using a full cartridge of caulk, the stuff won't stop coming out of the nozzle when you let go of the trigger. So as soon as your finger's off the trigger, release the notched plunger; this will relieve the pressure on the cartridge and you won't have a mess on your hands.

The caulk or glazing compound will take about a day to set. It won't get hard that fast—it takes a long time for that—but it will form a skin. Once this happens, give the sash a finish coat or two of paint and put them back in the frame. Just reverse the taking-out process: attach the cords to the upper sash, put in the parting bead with finishing nails, attach the cords to the lower sash, nail the sash peak in place.

You may, though, want to put new sash cords in. And in a lot of cases, you will find no sash cords when you take the window apart.

Installing New Sash Cords

On the inside of the frame, near the bottom, you will find removable pieces of wood. They may not be easy to spot right away because they've been painted over a dozen times, but if your window once had sash cords, these pieces of wood are there. They are usually held in place with screws. The screws may be so gunked up or rusted that they too are barely visible. Scrape them off as well as you can, then take your *old* screwdriver, put its blade in the screw slot at an angle, and tap it with your hammer until you clean the junk out of the slot. Then set the blade in the slot straight and give the screwdriver a couple of pretty hard shots with your hammer. Now take a good screwdriver and see if you can turn the screw. If not, go to work on it again with the old screwdriver until you can.

Take out the pieces of wood. There are pockets behind them.

In these pockets you should find the sash weights. But you probably won't, they were sold for scrap in World War II. If you do find them, you have the job of attaching new cords or chains to them, and it's a crummy one. You have to get the length of the cords just right. If they're too short, your window won't close all the way. If they're too long, it won't open easily.

If you've removed both sash, you'll put the upper one back first. There are two pulleys (the wheels I mentioned earlier) on each side of the window frame, up near the top. The outer pulleys are for the cords for the upper sash, the inner pulleys for the cords for the lower sash. Feed a new piece of sash cord over one of the outer pulleys and down to the weight in the pocket. Tie the cord to the weight. If you have trouble getting the cord down inside the frame, drop a string with a nail tied to it down first. Once you see the nail in the pocket, tie the other end of the string to your sash cord. Grab the nail and pull on the string until the cord appears in the pocket. Cut the string off the cord and tie the cord to the weight.

Okay, the weight is attached to the cord. Pull on the cord so that the weight comes right up against the pulley wheel. Set your sash on the windowsill and hold the new sash cord against it. The side of the sash should have a short groove near its top. This groove ends in a hole. Cut the cord 3 or 4 inches below this hole and tie a knot in it. Remove the sash from the sill and lean it against the wall.

Feed a cord over the other outer pulley, tie it to the weight, cut it to the same length as the first cord. Tie a knot in it. Set the sash on the sill again and push the knots of the cords into the holes in the sides of the sash. If there are no holes, or if the knots slip out, nail or staple the cords in place. (Use large wire fence staples, not the staple gun kind.) Position the sash in the frame, replace the parting bead, and see if the sash slides up and down okay. If it does, you've accomplished a miracle.

Once you have the upper sash in place, attach the lower sash in the same manner, and replace the sash peak.

This job obviously goes a lot better with two people: one to hold the sash and one to attach the cords. It goes better with two people, but it never seems to go really well.

A cautionary note: Don't try to use clothesline for sash cord. Sash cord may look like clothesline, but it's of much better quality. You can use sash chains if you want to mess with them. They never break, but they have a tendency to bunch up along the pulleys. Be sure to install them so they aren't twisted.

No matter how hard you work on windows like these, it is almost impossible to get them really tight and still have them function. For instance: your lower sash binds when you raise it, so you pry your sash peak off and move it out a bit. Then the first soft breeze comes along and the window starts to rattle. Or some such nonsense.

Fortunately, there's an alternative to the weight and pulley madness. Today, new sash are almost never installed with cords. They are installed with things called "sash balances." We'll get to these in a minute.

BUYING NEW SASH

Suppose your windows are really shot, or suppose some have 2 panes of glass, some 8, some 12, etc., and, loving consistency, you want to buy all new ones that are the same.

In Maine we were faced with some windows in pretty bad shape, and those in good shape didn't match each other. We decided to buy all new sash. Manufacturers still make sash that fit most window frames in old houses. (Curved tops and other such eccentricities are an exception.) Measure the inside dimensions of the frame from top to bottom and from side to side. Use a tape, and measure at the spot where the sash fit into the frame. If you have the old sash, measure them. Take the measurements to the lumberyard. You should be able to come pretty close to what you need.

We thought we were stuck on our upstairs windows. We wanted 6 over 6—one sash with 6 panes of glass (or "lights") on top of another sash the same, but we couldn't find a window this size. We finally realized that what we needed was 9 over 6. These sash fit the opening perfectly.

You may have to settle for sash just slightly smaller than your opening and build your frame out some with ¼" plywood, but don't order sash that are too big. You don't want to cut them down; you'll really get into a mess if you try.

INSTALLING NEW SASH

New double hung sash have grooves in their sides. These grooves are for the "sash balances" that I mentioned above. If you want to install new sash with cords and pulleys, you have to buy filler strips to nail into these grooves. Don't bother. Get rid of the old cords and pulleys and buy sash balances.

You've undoubtedly seen sash balances: they're those aluminum channels on the sides of the frames of new windows. There are two kinds: one has a sort of a tube for the sash to slide on, the other has fixed ridges of aluminum. You want the latter. The tubes can get screwed up, and the ones made out of plastic break. When you order your sash, order your balances too, they'll come in a size to fit the sash you're buying.

Until our house in Maine, I'd never installed sash balances. I really didn't know what to expect. I certainly never imagined that the job would be as easy as it was. Here's how you do it.

Take out the old sash, sash peak, and parting bead so that all you have left is the frame. That's all you will want. If the pulleys are still in place, remove them too.

Now you'll need some help. One person holds the balances upright, spaced as far apart as the sash is wide. For example, if the sash is 30″ wide, hold the balances 30″ apart. The balances are slanted on the bottom to fit the slant of the windowsill. Make sure the slants are facing in the right direction. From above, insert the bottom sash in the inside channel of the balances, and the upper sash in the outside channel. Push both sash down about halfway into the balances. They will catch on the springs behind the aluminum ridges, and you'll feel the tension.

Have your helper keep holding one balance, and you hold the other. Keep them pressed tightly against the sash so that the sash don't slip. Carefully coordinating your efforts, lift this whole unit into place in the window frame. There is a board or piece of trim on the outside of the frame. This used to hold the upper sash in place. The outside edges of the balances go right up against this trim and their bottoms rest on the windowsill. Once they are in this position they will stay there pretty much by themselves, but it's good to have your helper keep a steadying hand on the sash.

Make sure both balances are snug and straight against the trim, then nail a 4d nail right through the aluminum of each balance and into the wood of the frame. Nail either in the lower part of the outer channel or the upper part of the inner channel, but don't hammer the nails in all the way because you may still want to make some adjustments. (Nail through the flat part of the balance, of course, not through one of the protruding ridges.)

The window should now stay in place. Test to see how the sash slide. If they are too loose, put little shims between the balance and the frame until the sash slide up and down and stay where you put them. Then nail a few more 4d nails through the balances, anchoring them in place. You need only about 4 nails in each balance. Drive the nails in all the way with a nail set (see glossary). (A large nail hit on the wrong end will serve just as well.) Be *careful* when you nail: these balances are delicate, and one good hammer blow can mess the ridges up badly.

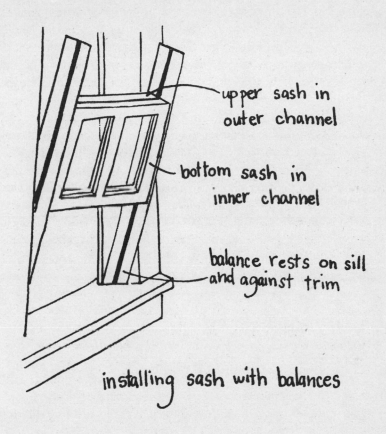

upper sash in
outer channel

bottom sash in
inner channel

balance rests on sill
and against trim

installing sash with balances

Sash balances have two main advantages over the old fashioned cords and pulleys. First, they are far easier to install. Secondly, they give you a window that's really tight—no rattling sash with these.

What are their disadvantages? Well, it may take some sophisticated shimming to get the window to stay open at every point along the balance and still not bind. When you do get it just right, you may find that when the weather changes, your window either sticks or won't stay shut unless you keep the catch on. The other problem is that if you should ever want to remove a sash, you'll have to take the whole balance out. You do this by chopping away the aluminum around the nails, which will probably mean the end of your balance. But in my opinion, the advantages of the balances far outweigh the disadvantages.

Now suppose you have old sash in good shape, or in renewable shape, and you don't want to mess with weights and cords. These old sash aren't grooved on the sides, so you can't use standard balances. If you have a router or know someone who has, it's possible to cut some grooves. But there are now balances made especially for these old, ungrooved sash. They are a relatively new development, and you will probably have to order them. Your lumberyard may never have heard of them, but they do exist, so keep trying. I haven't used them, but if they're as good as the standard balances, I'd take them any day over messing with weights and cords.

SASH GLIDES

Suppose you're in an old apartment where the windows don't work. The weights and cords are gone, and the sash just slide against the trim. I'd stick the top sash in place and forget about it. Drive nails or small blocks of wood into the frame to keep the sash all the way up, and run some rope caulk around it so it doesn't leak air. You want the bottom sash to operate, so pick up some sash glides. There are different kinds on the market. They are just pieces of spring metal that slip in between the sash and the frame and are nailed into the top of the sash. They let the sash slide up and down (sort of) and make it stay where you want it (almost), and you don't have to take the window apart to install them.

STORM WINDOWS

If you don't use sash balances, which provide a very snug fit for the sash, you should definitely install aluminum storm windows, because the old wooden double hung windows are going to leak air no matter what you do. Even if you do use balances, you should consider storm windows. They keep the house cleaner, quieter, save a lot of heat (there's almost twice as much heat loss through a single pane of glass as through a double pane), help retain humidity, and help preserve your sash and frame by protecting them from the weather. They also prevent ice and condensation on the inside of your window; this moisture can ruin your paint and even the sash itself. Storm windows are a very worthwhile investment.

Home Made Storm Sash

You can make an inexpensive storm sash out of 1 x 3 pine boards. Be sure to measure each window that you make one for, because in an old place each window will be different. Hold the

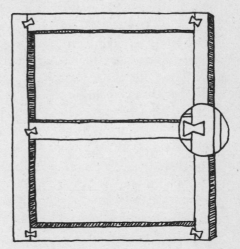

frame and the crosspiece together with "Skotch" wood fasteners. You just hammer these into the surface of the boards at each corner, and they make a tight joint. Staple 4 mil polyethelene plastic over the frame. For a couple of dollars, you've got a storm window.

The disadvantages of this kind of sash are: the plastic will eventually rip or deteriorate, you can't see through it well, and there's no tight seal between the sash and the window frame— unless you caulk it, but you don't want to do that because in the spring you'll want to take it down and put up a screen. You also have to have a place to store it in the summer. And if you want some fresh air on a winter day, you'll have to go outside. If you plan to stay for a while, buy the aluminum windows with built-in screens. But if you're not staying long or you're in an apartment, this kind of thing can save a good amount of heat and make you a lot more comfortable.

WEATHERSTRIPPING

If you don't have aluminum storm sash and your windows are old, you ought at least to weatherstrip them. An awful lot of cold air can come through them on a windy day. You should also weatherstrip around your doors, whether or not you have storm doors.

The spring bronze strips work well on doors, and so do the wood strips edged with foam and the metal strips edged with vinyl. Felt is terrible: it mats down with pressure and soon loses its effectiveness.

You can make a good weatherstrip on metal casement windows by running a bead of silicone sealer around the frame where it meets the sash. This will give a tight seal and should hold up for several years.

OLD DOORS

Doors are expensive. I always try to pick up old ones if I can. A new inside door will cost about six times as much as a used one, and the price of a new exterior door is out of sight. I've often been able to get old doors in good condition for nothing or very little. While doors are worth a mint new, they depreciate even faster than mobile homes.

It's understandable. It's hard to get a bunch of doors of the same design unless you buy out someone's whole house, the doors have depressions and holes where the old hinges and locksets used to be, they have been cut to fit a particular opening, etc. Some old doors are warped, and these you want to avoid—trying to get them to close right will drive you crazy. But if a door is solid and straight and the right design and size, buy it. If it's coming apart at the top or bottom, glue will do the job, especially epoxy. You may even find that the existing mortises are right for some hinges you have on hand or can buy, and you can save yourself half your mortising job. If the door has a lockset that you can use, or has a mortise for a lock that you can buy, you really have saved yourself a job. (But if the lock mortise isn't right, you'll have to fill it with a block of wood.)

ADDING A PIECE TO A DOOR

A lot of old doors are shorter than the standard door of today. I guess that's because people used to be shorter, but I really don't know. Today's doors are usually not any shorter than 6'-8", but old doors are often 6'-6" or less. If you see an old door like this that matches one in your house you can always add a piece to the bottom. You'll need a piece of wood as thick as the door,

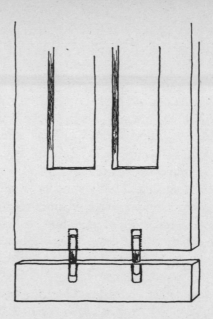

and the best place to get that is from another old door that was in such bad shape that someone threw it away.

Cut a piece of wood the proper length and depth, lay your door flat on the floor and put the piece up against it. About 6″ in from the sides, make marks on both the door and the extension. Drill centered, ⅜″ wide holes into the bottom of the door and the extension at these points. Make the holes 2″ deep. Then attach the extension to the door bottom with 4″ long pieces of ⅜″ dowel, coating the dowels and the bottom of the door with glue. Tap the extension with a hammer until it fits snugly against the edge of the door, wipe off the excess glue, and you're all set.

HANGING A DOOR

In my opinion, hanging a door is one of the most distasteful home repair jobs of all. The truth is, I have never yet met anyone

who liked to hang doors. I met one guy new to the home
remodeling field who said he didn't *mind* hanging doors, but I
never met anyone who said he liked it. I would say to forget it,
that this is one spot to admit that you're licked and call in a pro,
but then I'm afraid you would have a lot of doors that never got
hung. If hanging doors is part of an extensive remodeling job, of
course a carpenter will do it, but I have never succeeded in
getting a man out just to hang a door, or even a number of
doors. If somebody specialized in this, he (or she) would have no
end of business.

Obviously there must be a reason for this state of affairs.
There is: hanging a door in an old house is tricky, unpredictable,
tedious, and frustrating. You just never know how the job will
turn out. Quite frankly, it's easier to hang yourself, and after you
read this, you'll probably want to.

Avoid it if You Can

I'll never forget my first attempt at door hanging. On Lawrence
Street we had a door that led from the first floor hallway out to
the alley. The hallway was dark and the old door was beat up
and rotten, so we thought it would be nice to replace it with a
new door with glass panes. I bought a very nice brand new door
at an exorbitant price, picked up a pair of new hinges, and,
figuring I might need some help, called my friend Vince and
asked if he could come over Saturday morning. It shouldn't take
very long, all we had to do was take down the old door and put
up the new one in the very same spot, and then we could go
shopping, go to the park, go to the art museum, go . . .

To repeat, the first thing to remember about hanging a door is
to avoid it if you possibly can. It took us the entire day. And
when the sun sank slowly and mockingly in the west, the lousy
door still wasn't right. As a matter of fact, I never *did* get it right.

In old places, over the years the door jambs have settled and
twisted and the doors have gone right along with them like

partners in perverse marriages, and after all the sinking and bending, they still close and latch. But try to team up a proud new straight door with that old jamb, and oh brother.

So take a good look at this door that you want to replace, and see if you can do something to keep it. Maybe it swings okay, but it's all gunked up with paint and crud. Maybe it has a cracked panel. Can't you scrape that stuff off, can't you patch that panel with water putty and tape? (Use the rubberized crack-sealing tape I mentioned in the "cracks" section of the chapter on walls. Savogran water putty is the best I've come across.) Maybe the hinge screws have pulled out of the frame and the door falls on your foot each time you open it. Coat pieces of toothpick with glue and jam them into the old screw holes until they're packed tight. Let the glue harden and screw the hinges back in place, using screws slightly larger than the originals. Maybe the door doesn't latch. This too may be caused by loose hinges. If not, see if you can reset the strike plate (the thing the latch goes into), or even put in a whole new lockset, but try, please try not to take that old door down and put in a new one.

Sometimes, though, you'll have to. Sometimes the door will be bashed beyond all hope. Or maybe you want glass panes instead of what you have, or you want to get rid of glass panes, or maybe the existing door is a homemade collage of plywood and moldings that for some reason does not appeal to you. Or maybe the door has simply disappeared. Okay, you're in for it.

The Old Door Jamb

First consider the door jamb carefully. You will be incredibly fortunate if you can work with the one you have. In almost every case you will find something wrong with it: it isn't square, it isn't plumb, it's twisted so that it sticks out more at the top than at the bottom. It's an odd size, and no new door you can buy will fit. Etc.

The really important thing is that the jamb be plumb on both sides. Sometimes a few wood wedges will let you plumb up the existing jamb, but usually not. Often you have to tear out the existing jamb and put in a new one. Okay, it's a job, but it could be worse. The point is, unless you are highly skilled, you'll never get your door to work right without a plumb jamb, and replacement is well worth it.

If the jamb is not square, you can always cut your door off crooked at the top so that it fits, but do you want to do that? If the jamb is twisted, replace it.

Often the wall in which the jamb sits has a lean to it. If you hang your door on one side of a wall such as this, it won't stay closed unless it's latched, and you may not be able to open it all the way because after a point it scrapes against the floor. If you hang the door on the other side of this wall, you will have to open it uphill, against gravity, and it won't stay open. It's nice to have the door run straight up and down, but it isn't crucial. Having the sides of the jamb plumb is.

Making a New Door Jamb

Making a new door jamb may sound like a tremendous job, but it isn't all that bad. In general, you can simply cover the short studs and the header around the door opening (see fig. p. 51) with 1″ (¾″ thick) pine finish boards. Before we get to the details, let's rule out a couple of other possibilities.

Instead of making your jamb out of 1″ boards, you could buy ready-made jamb stock and make it out of that. Your existing warped or crooked jamb is probably made of such stock. It's cut so that you don't need a separate stop molding, the strip of wood that runs around the inside of the jamb and meets the edge of your door when it's closed. But in an old place you may find that once you have the new door hung, you want to move the stop one way or the other for a better fit, and with ready-made jamb stock you can't do it. A second reason why I

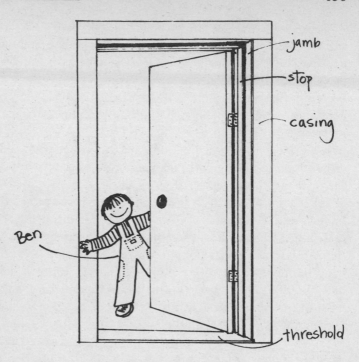

like the jamb made of 1″ boards and separate stop molding better than I like the ready-made—it's cheaper.

Another alternative is to buy a door that comes already hung in a jamb. You just set these pre-hung units in place with shims and nail them into the short studs. The trouble is, most pre-hung doors are not very beautiful. They come with their casing (the trim around them) built in, and you'll surely have trouble finding a match for anything old.

So here's how to make the new jamb yourself: First, tear out the old jamb. When you do, you may find that there aren't any short studs along its sides. In old construction, a ready-made jamb was sometimes simply nailed into the floor and header. That's how the jambs were installed in the house I live in now. If you run into this situation in your place, you'll have to frame in the doorway with studs in the manner described in the section on building a partition. The old jamb was quite thick and sturdy, but ours will just be 1″ boards, and we need a firm backing.

Once the framing is adequate, cover it with 1″ thick pine finish boards. Use boards that are wide enough to come out flush with the finished wall surface on both sides of the wall. For example, if the studs in the wall are 2½″ wide and they are covered on each side with ½″ plasterboard, the total thickness of the wall is 3½″. So you want to use 1 x 4 (really ¾″ x 3½″) boards for your jamb. Put the top piece of wood in first. Then put in the side pieces, shimming them out so they're plumb (if necessary). Nail the boards in tightly with 8d finishing nails. Make sure you use #2 grade or better boards. Today's #3 boards are so full of knots that it will be hard to find clear places to put your hinges.

If you're going to have a threshold (or "saddle"), put it in now. You can buy a ready-made threshold at the lumberyard, or make one yourself. Plane off the edges of a 1″ thick board so it will slope gradually on each side of the door (then you won't catch your shoe on it). You should use something tough like yellow pine, because it will receive a lot of wear. Cut it to fit tightly between the sides of the jamb, and secure it with two nails driven into each end. Drill pilot holes for the nails to keep them from splitting the wood. If you put down the threshold *before* you install your jamb, you'll have to cut the bottoms of the 1″ boards in a curve to fit around the curve of the threshold. This is hard.

Once the threshold is in, it's time to install the stop. There are all kinds of stops: some are absolutely plain, just flat thin boards, others are fancy in varying degrees. They are usually ⅜″ or so thick, and they come in different widths. Ask your lumberyard to show you the kinds of door stops they carry. If they show you little rubber wedges to hold your door open, explain that you want the molding that runs around the inside of a jamb. If you have the money, pick what suits your fancy. If you're hard up and don't care to get elaborate, you can have a

1″ pine board (¾″ thick, remember) cut into ½″ wide strips. This will give you a stop ¾″ x ½″, perfectly adequate, but not elegant.

Now take a look at the hinges you're going to use to hang your door. You'll see that they have two leaves held together by a removable pin. Measure the width of one leaf (the width of both leaves is the same) and deduct ¹⁄₁₆″ from this measurement. For example: Let's suppose you use the common 3½″ x 3½″ hinge. One leaf of this hinge is 1½″ wide. Deduct ¹⁄₁₆″ from this width and you have 1⁷⁄₁₆″.

Next, decide on which side of the jamb you are going to hang your door. From this side, measure in from the edge of the jamb this 1⁷⁄₁₆″ (if your hinge leaf is 1½″ wide), and mark the inside of the jamb at this point. Mark it at both the top and the bottom. Mark the piece of jamb on the opposite side of the doorway in the same manner—1⁷⁄₁₆″ in from the edge. Your stop will be nailed to the jamb along these markings.

Now measure up from the top of the threshold to the top of the jamb. You should have 6′-8¼″ if you've done the job

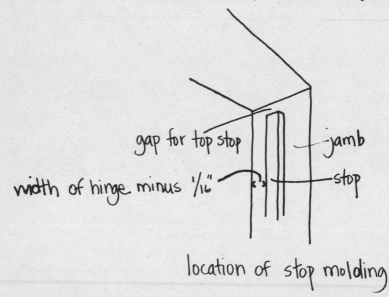

perfectly, but you'd better check just to make sure. (Nobody's perfect.) Cut two pieces of stop to this length, *minus* the thickness of the stop itself. In other words, if the height is 6'-8¼" and the thickness of the stop is ⅜", cut two pieces of stop 6'-7⅞" long. (The ⅜" gap at the top is for the top stop, which will be nailed in later.) Rest the stop on the threshold and line its inside edge up with the marks you made on the jamb. In the above example, you would have 1⁷⁄₁₆" between the edge of the jamb and the edge of the stop. Nail the stop in place temporarily with 4d finishing nails. Just use a couple of nails and don't drive them in all the way, you may have to move the stop later.

With the side stop in place, you have something to lean your door against while you try to hang it. Except for the top stop, your frame is now finished.

Check to see that your old door is square. If it's not (it won't be), saw it or plane it square. Now comes the fun part.

Butt Hinges, I

The thing almost universally used to hang doors, the thing we are all familiar with is the "butt hinge." (At the hardware store, just ask for a pair of 3½" butts.) They are a fine device and work quite well if you get one little troublesome detail just right: the mortise. Look at a door. Notice that the surface of the hinges is flush with the edge of the door and also flush with the casing. It is flush because the hinges have been set into little depressions the thickness of the hinge. These depressions are known as the mortises.

In order for the butt hinge to work right, these mortises must be cut to the exact depth of the hinge. If that hinge is ³⁄₃₂" thick, that mortise had better be ³⁄₃₂" thick too, or you're in trouble. As you can imagine, that exactness is not easy to come by. It takes good eyes, good hands, patience and time. Cutting mortises is the big reason people don't like to hang doors. I'll describe how to do it, but first . . .

If mortises were absolutely necessary, well, you'd grin and bear it. But the amazing truth is they are not absolutely necessary, because of a simple and delightful invention called the no-mortise hinge.

A Digression: The Elusive No-Mortise Hinge

The no-mortise hinge has an offset built right into its leaves: this eliminates the need to sink it below the surface of the door and jamb. You just screw it right on without cutting anything, and it works. There is only one problem with it—it's almost impossible to find.

I read about no-mortise hinges years ago. Fantastic, I thought, the answer to an amateur's prayer, I'll run right down to the hardware store and pick up a pair and hang that dreaded third door. (Dreaded because the first and second hangings had been such miserable failures.) I went through an involved explanation, then answered the inevitable, "Well what do you want that for?" It looked as if you couldn't get the things without a prescription. An extensive, mocking search of the hinge department disclosed, much to the salesman's surprise, a few pairs of small, thin, flimsy-looking things that reminded me of butterflies. "This what you want?" the guy asked.

It said no-mortise on the box, so, "Yeah, that's it," I said with false assurance.

"Wonder who ordered these?" the guy said. "Never seen 'em around here before. Don't get much call for this kind of stuff, most people use butts."

With an eagerness enhanced by a sense of doing something forbidden, I hung my door. It was a thin, light thing and it's good it was: the hinges were certainly not strong enough to hold anything substantial. The door didn't close just perfectly, but it did close, and considering the fact that it was warped and hung in a crooked frame, I was quite pleased. It sure worked an awful lot better than the other two doors I'd hung.

I didn't have occasion to hang another door for several years. At last I was faced with the dreaded task again. But this time I went to the hardware store (a different one) full of confidence. Surely in all this time no-mortise hinges had made great strides, were common items in hardware stores across the land, had even replaced butt hinges to a great extent. But a check of the store's shelves revealed—no no-mortise hinges at all, and brought forth my first "What do you want them for?" of the afternoon. There were none in the next closest hardware store either, so off I went across town to the place where I'd bought them the first time. They had some—the same flimsy things they'd had four years before, probably some of the same stock. The door I wanted to hang was pretty heavy, and I figured I'd need about fifteen of these little jobs to hold it properly. That would lead to too many questions from the neighbors, friends, insurance salesmen, etc., not to mention peals of derisive laughter. I abandoned my search temporarily, left my door unhung, had mortise nightmares.

About a month later I was wandering through the hardware department of the Sears store in Camden, New Jersey, and bong—I couldn't believe my eyes. Not just one, but several sizes of no-mortise hinges, real, honest-to-goodness thick brass-plated beauties for hanging real honest-to-goodness doors! Exulting, I bought a pair of 3½ inchers.

They worked great. The door worked great (considering its warp). That was it, my problem was solved forever, the mighty Sears had seen the light.

The next time I had to hang a door I went to Sears (in Moorestown, N.J., they had moved from Camden), looked through the hardware display—and found not one no-mortise hinge. A panicky feeling claimed my left lung as I approached the salesman. No, they didn't carry them. No, they did not plan to carry them. When they moved from Camden they cut down on the size of the hardware department and eliminated certain items from their inventory. Would they have them at other Sears stores? I asked. He wouldn't know. What did I want them for anyway?

I have never found them again. I have found some of the flimsy ones—and a word of warning here—I have also gotten stuck. I bought some rather frail-looking 3″ no-mortise hinges in desperation, figuring I could make do with them, only to discover too late that they had no removable pins. They are for hinging together folding doors. Watch out. You can't use these to hang a regular door. Well, I guess you can, but I wouldn't try it.

Off and on I continue my search. I have learned to cope with the butt hinge now, but mortising seems like such a waste of time, and even though you're terribly careful, sometimes you just can't get it right. I pine for the no-mortise hinge. Maybe you'll have better luck in your search than I've had, but I doubt it.

Butt Hinges, II

Okay, let's suppose you don't find the no-mortise hinge. How do you hang your door? You'll need: a pair of 3½″ butt hinges, sharp pencil, wedges (see below), ice pick or awl, screwdriver, pocket knife, and the world's sharpest wood chisel. Before you begin, take a good look at a door that's already hung. Keep going back to this door whenever you get confused.

You've got your jamb up, you've got your stop in place. Next you want to position your door in the opening, allowing ⅛″ at the top and both sides, and ⅜″ at the bottom. Stick a piece of ⅜″ thick wood on the threshold, lift your door up on top of this and push it against the stop. Hold it there with wedges (little shims of wood shingle or cardboard) while you mark the spot where your top hinge will go. If you have a helper, you won't need the wedges.

Measure 7″ down from the top of the door. With a *sharp* pencil, make a mark on both the door and the jamb. Your top

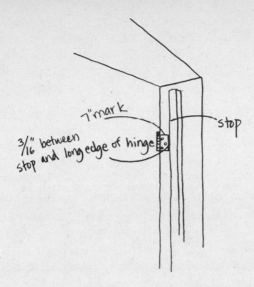

3/16" between stop and long edge of hinge

7" mark

stop

marking the location of the top hinge of the jamb

hinge will go just below this mark. (If there's a knot in the jamb at this spot, you'll have to move the mark up so the hinge won't fall on the knot. Mortising is bad enough without knots.) Remove the door from the opening.

Take a hinge, hold it pin up, and place its top edge on the inside of the jamb at the 7" mark. Set its long edge $\frac{3}{16}$" back from the stop molding.

Take a pencil and trace around the hinge. Mark the thickness of the hinge (usually $\frac{3}{32}$") on the edge of the jamb, because the depth of the cutout is critical.

Take your pocket knife and score the hinge outline you've drawn on the jamb. Score as deep or deeper than the thickness of the hinge.

Now you'll need that incredibly sharp wood chisel. What you want to do is *pare* this mortise out with the chisel, just using the pressure of your hands. If you hit the chisel with a hammer or mallet you are almost sure to cut too deeply and botch things up, so, very slowly, push the chisel into the wood, just shaving pieces off, until you have an even, level depression the exact size and depth of the hinge. Sounds like fun, huh? But if you go easy and don't bite off too much at a time, you'll probably be okay. Hold your hinge up to the job from time to time so you don't get carried away and pare off too much.*

The top mortise has been cut into the jamb. Now stand your door on edge with the edge that will take the latchset on the floor and the edge to be mortised for hinges facing up. Lay a hinge on the edge of the door, again pin up. Put the top edge of the hinge at the 7″ mark, and set the long edge back from the edge of the door ⅛″. The setback is toward the side of the door that faces the stop.

Mark the hinge outline on the door and mortise it. Be sure you're mortising the right edge of the door! Hold the door up to the jamb again if you get confused.

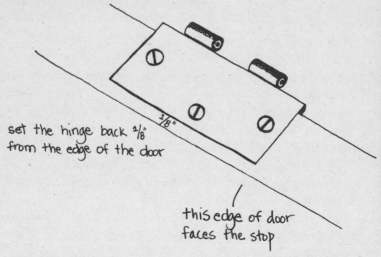

set the hinge back ⅛″ from the edge of the door

⅛″

this edge of door faces the stop

* Flash: Recently I saw an ad for a thing called an "electri-chisel," an attachment for an electric drill which will cut a mortise to just the right size and depth with, so they say, no sweat. I haven't used it, but it would be worth looking into.

Now mark the location of your bottom door mortise. Measure 8″ up from the bottom of the door. Lay the *bottom* edge of your second hinge at this mark, set the long edge back ⅛″ from the edge of the door, draw around the hinge and cut the mortise.

Now, back to the upper hinge. Hold the hinge up to the mortise in the top of the jamb. Be sure the pin is up, and screw the appropriate leaf to the jamb. There's a hole underneath the hinge where the two leaves meet. Stick a nail in this hole, tap it with a hammer, and remove the hinge pin, separating the hinge leaves. Screw the other hinge leaf to the mortise in the top of the door.

Now screw the appropriate leaf of the other hinge to the bottom door mortise, take out the pin, and separate the leaves. Lay this remaining hinge leaf aside for the moment.

Set the door in place in the jamb, top hinge leaves meeting, and put the top hinge pin in about ⅔ of the way. One of your bottom hinge leaves is screwed to the door. Mark its location on the bottom of the jamb. Remove the door. Pick up your remaining hinge leaf and draw its outline on the bottom of the jamb between the marks you've just made. Remember to set the long edge of the hinge 3/16″ back from the stop. Cut the mortise. Screw the remaining hinge leaf to this mortise.

Put the door back in place. The leaves of both hinges should mesh. If you had marked and mortised the bottom of the jamb earlier, before you had the top hinge up, you'd probably find at this point that the bottom hinge leaves would *not* mesh. Put in the top hinge pin first, then the bottom hinge pin.

The door should now swing perfectly. It may not. If you've cut any of the mortises too deep, you can shim them out with thin pieces of cardboard. If you haven't cut them deep enough, you'll have to take the hinge off and go at it again. If you don't have the hinges screwed on straight, you'll have to align them. Adjust the stops if they need it, and nail them and the top stop into place permanently.

Now suppose you've been lucky enough to find no-mortise

hinges. You follow the same procedure as above, except you just draw the outline of the hinges on the jamb and door, forget the mortising and screw them right on. Just a little bit simpler, right?

You still have to install your latch set. Latch sets come with instruction sheets. These are usually confusing, but I'm sure my confusion is as great as yours, and anything I'd have to say would make things worse.

One encouraging note: I do a pretty good job hanging doors now, and I really don't mind it. The first dozen are the hardest. So—cheer up.

8 YOUR FLOORS

WOOD FLOORS

YOUR OLD PLACE IS LIKELY TO HAVE A GEM OF A LIVING ROOM floor—in the rough, of course. It may have random width boards of pine, spruce, oak or some other nice thing. In its rough state, it may look disastrous, but unless it's really smashed and broken, you can refinish it and make it look better than you or anyone else ever dreamed.

There is probably no other remodeling job as satisfying as taking a drab, beat-up, nondescript wooden floor and sanding and finishing it into a thing of beauty. The results are always dramatic, often incredible. We couldn't believe how well our floors turned out on Lawrence Street, on Lambert Street, and especially on Wallston Road, where the boards were warped and splintery and riddled with hatchet cuts. In each house the floors were finished in a different way, and in each case they turned out looking great.

But before you refinish your floors, you will have to repair them. There may be loose and broken boards, large cracks, or boards that don't match others.

Loose Boards

Loose boards should be nailed into the joists with 10d or 12d galvanized finishing nails. Floors in old houses commonly have just one layer of boards, and you can usually tell where the joists are by observing the rows of nails that run across the floor.

But not always: sometimes a second layer of boards has been laid on top of the original, and it has simply been nailed into the old boards instead of into the joists. So in this case, the nailing pattern you observe has nothing to do with where the joists are. These newer boards often become loose and squeaky, and it's best to fasten them to the joists too. But how can you find the joists in a case like this?

If you are working on the first floor, you can go down into the cellar and note the pattern of the joists (if there *is* a pattern)— 18″ on center, for example. Drill a tiny hole up through the floor beside one joist and put a little wire through it as a marker. Once this joist is located in the room above, keep measuring at 18″ intervals across the floor and drive nails in at these spots.

On the second and third floors, of course, you can't observe the joists (unless you've torn out the ceiling below), so you're in for a bit of trial and error. Just hope the joists are evenly spaced.

Some tips: If you have a soft pine floor, you may have to use a nail with a bigger head than a finishing nail, because the small head may go right through the board. A galvanized box nail will work fine. And when the end of a board is loose, again—drill pilot holes to keep the nails from splitting the wood.

Diving Boards

Sometimes you'll encounter the diving board syndrome: the end of a floorboard falls short of a joist, and there's nothing to nail it into. Here you have to pry up the board and build out the joist with pieces of wood in order to give yourself a nailing base. Nail these wood cleats on firmly. Drill pilot holes and drive several good-sized nails through them. Even with this, years of walking can work the cleats loose. For a more permanent job, screw them on.

Old Wood

If you're going to sand your floor, try to replace broken boards with old wood, because you'll never get new wood to blend with the old. Maybe there will be some old boards lying around the place or maybe you can pick some up at a salvage company. An old piece of white pine will blend in better with old yellow pine boards than a new piece of yellow pine. You try to get the same kind of wood that's in your floor, of course, but sometimes you can't find it.

Taking Up Old Boards

Old floors are usually quite dry and brittle. When you remove a board to replace it or whatever, pry under each nail a little at a time, loosening the entire length of board, and then go back and pry up under each nail again until you can take it out. If you aren't gentle and patient, you'll break the board. If the board is tongue-and-groove (see glossary), you'll probably break it no matter how careful you are. Worse, you may break the groove bead of the board next to the one you're taking out. Then you'll want to take that one up, and then . . . It's a good idea to chop off the tongue of this kind of board before you remove it. Stick a chisel in the crack between the boards, hit it with a hammer, and cut the tongue off. Then maybe you can get the board up without wrecking any others. If the chisel blade is too thick to fit in the crack, sharpen a stiff putty knife and use that.

Take up a board only when it's really necessary, and hope that your electrician will do the same.

Spaces

Old floors often have large spaces between the boards. This adds to their charm. These spaces fill up over the years with dirt and cat fur and don't look bad when the floor is sealed. Sometimes, though, you'll have a really wide gap—$\frac{3}{8}''$ or more—that you'll want to fill with something else.

If there's a subfloor—something under the finish floor to provide some backing—you'll be tempted to fill the crack with putty. This may hold up for a number of years, but someday it will work loose. It may hold up for only a month or two if the boards have any give to them. You can use linseed oil putty or water putty (a dry powder that you mix with water), but the results will be the same, fair to poor. I've read that you can mix sawdust with waterproof glue and use it as a filler. This should hold better, but I've never tried it.

There is, however, a crack filler that will work: paste epoxy. This is a very dark gray, almost black, and cracks filled with it look pretty much like any other cracks in your old floor. This stuff holds incredibly well: I've even had it hold "diving boards" in place. It is expensive and rather messy to work with. I wouldn't do a whole floor with it, but for a small area, especially where you want holding power as well as filler, you can't beat it.

Lots of old places have no subfloor. We had none on Lawrence or Lambert. When you had a gap in the boards on the first floor of those houses, you were looking into the cellar. In cases like these, there's only one thing to do: cut a strip of wood to fit the gap and nail it in place. Coat the sides of the strip with glue, and drive small finishing nails into the joists at an angle. Cut the strip thick enough so that it comes up higher than the existing floor (you may have to use two strips, one on top of the other), then plane it level. (Sink your nails first!)

Even if there's a subfloor, this is the best way to fill your cracks. But you should know that it is a tedious, time-consuming method, and professionals today almost never use it. (If they do, they will charge you a fortune.) They will use putty instead, and will tell you quite frankly that it will not hold up.

There may be some small holes in your boards where old electric wires used to go. You can fill these with glue-coated corks.

Persistent Squeaks

Some boards will squeak no matter what you do. You use screws to hold them down instead of nails, countersinking them and covering the heads with wood filler or putty; you go down to the cellar and screw up into them through the subfloor; you squirt graphite or silicone into their cracks. No good; they persist. Unless you want to tear up some floor (always trouble), you'll have to live with them.

But not all boards are so persistent. Fortunately, just by renailing, you will be able to cut down drastically on the amount of backtalk from your floor.

SANDING YOUR FLOOR

Some people like to water ski, some like to snowmobiling. I prefer floor sanding because it combines the best features of both: fantastic din and the sense of being dragged helplessly across wide open spaces. It is hard to anticipate the pull a floor sanding machine exerts. The thing looks sort of like an upright vacuum cleaner, and you might think it isn't much harder to handle. If you think this, you are wrong.

When you sand a floor, have at least two people on hand. Three is better and four is better still. The machine not only grinds down your floor, it grinds you down too.

If the floor is really rough and chewed up, think twice before you do the job yourself. The sanders used by the pros are much bigger and heavier than those you rent, so heavy that they are brought into your house in pieces and assembled on the job. These machines can cope with a really bad floor. You'll have a tough time getting really bad floors level with a rental machine. If you have any doubts, get an estimate from a floor man, he'll tell you what's involved.

The rental machine will be plenty heavy enough for you to handle, though. Getting it into your car will snap your spine, and taking it up a flight of stairs will give you the thrill of your life.

When you rent a machine, the guy at the paint store will ask you what kind of wood your floor is made of, how big the room is, and what the floor is covered with (paint, varnish, etc.). He will give you more than enough sandpaper to do the job; you pay only for what you use and return the rest. Usually he gives you coarse, medium, and fine papers. He'll show you how to attach them to the sander's drum. He will also rent you an edger, a small circular sander that lets you do the corners and edges of the floor. By the way, if you have only a small area to do, consider renting just an edger. You do risk gouging some circles into your boards, but the machine is relatively easy to control, easy to lift, and it will do a perfectly decent job if you use several grades of paper and take your time.

Before you start sanding, you have to sink all nail heads below the surface of the floor with a nail set and hammer. Or else. I neglected this detail the first time I sanded. Our friend Jack proudly gave us a lesson in the use of the machine: halfway across the room his sandpaper blew to shreds. We puzzled over the explosion but couldn't explain it. We loaded up again and POW! same thing. We must've lost ten papers and spent a thousand curses on that sander when we finally realized what was wrong. Once we sank the nails, the trouble ended.

Start with the coarse paper. Keep the sander moving steadily down the floor in the direction in which the floorboards run. If you stop, you'll put a hollow in your boards. When you come to a high spot that needs leveling, go back and forth over it, but keep moving. With a rental machine you may have to go *across* the grain to grind a board down even with the others. This will make marks that you'll have to erase by going over the spot again the right way.

The tricky part comes when you reach the end of the room and have to turn around. Don't stop, just keep going and make the turn as smoothly and evenly as possible. When you tire, have a helper cut in and take the machine from you while you're still moving. Don't ever let the machine sit in one spot while it's running.

Every 15 minutes or so you will want to stop the machine. Tilt it backwards, turn off the switch, and wait for the drum to stop revolving before you put it down on the floor again. You will want to stop the machine because the noise is driving you crazy, the sawdust bag is full—and the thing is drawing a lot of current through your wiring system.

Wiring is an important consideration in running a sander. If you have #12 wire in your outlets you may be okay, but if you have #14, you are going to have to stop the sander now and then and let your wiring cool off. No matter what size wire you have, be sure not to have anything else drawing power from the circuit that you have the sander plugged into. We had #14 wire in our living room on Lawrence Street. We had nothing else drawing on the circuit while we did the floor, but after one rather long stretch of work, the sander went dead. First the popping sandpaper, then this, and a groan rose from the crowd. We were sure we'd broken the thing, but then we found we'd merely tripped a circuit breaker.

We had a beer and let the machine and the wires and ourselves cool off, and then I went down to the cellar and flipped the breaker on. Above my head came a roar, screams, a crash, then silence. We'd forgotten to turn off the switch on the sander. So when I turned the power on, the thing shot over the floor like a tank, bashed a piece out of the wall and cracked the baseboard. We were happy when the job was done and the monster was out of our home.

Do the whole floor once with the coarse paper, once with the medium, and once with the fine. Do the fine sanding in your socks, so you won't mar the new surface with your shoes. Do the edges with the edger, again in three steps. Use a light touch and you won't grind your periphery too full of circles. There is a little patch in each corner of the room that the edger won't reach. You'll have to sand these spots by hand.

Finishes

You want to put a finish on your floor right after you sand it. Otherwise you'll surely get it dirty, and chances are good that this dirt will show when the job is done. Before you put down the finish, sweep up and vacuum and get the floor as free of dust as you can.

On Lawrence Street our floors were a mellow, rich yellow pine. Davene finished them simply, with boiled linseed oil thinned with turpentine. She just brushed it on and let it soak in. (You thin the oil so it penetrates better and dries faster.) Once the oil dried, she paste-waxed the floors and buffed them. (You can rent a large disc sander for the buffing operation.) These floors looked terrific, but there are problems with this finish: Water will stain it, and it picks up a lot of dirt. (One friend of ours swears by tung oil. This gives a beautiful finish and is quite water resistant as well. We haven't used it, so I don't know if it picks up dirt.)

On Lambert Street we had our floors done for us. Again they were yellow pine. But there we had the men brush on a penetrating stain, then apply paste wax. We stained the floors because they'd been butchered over the years; all sorts of odds and ends of boards had been put down, including new ones, and we wanted a uniform appearance. Only a stain could give us this. This treatment looked great too, and it didn't pick up the dirt that the oiled floors did. The trouble with any waxed floor, of course, is that every so often you have to rewax and buff, and that's work. This also means buying or renting a machine, unless you want to buff by hand, and I don't think you do.

Our Wallston Road floors were really in tough shape, and we knew it would take a pro with his heavy machine to do the job right. Again we wanted them stained because of their poor condition. We wanted a color slightly different from those available, so our man took a *gloss* polyurethane varnish, added several tubes of oil color to it, and came up with what we had in mind. (He used yellow ochre, raw sienna, and burnt umber to make a pecan color.) He brushed this varnish onto the newly sanded floor, staining and sealing in one operation, and let the stuff dry overnight. The next day he buffed the floor with a steel wool pad on a large disc sander, then brushed on a coat of *satin* polyurethane varnish. This gave us a finish that looks almost exactly like wax. But it doesn't collect any dirt, never has to be buffed, and is extremely tough: water won't hurt it at all. It's the finish I'd recommend.

If you have oak or other open-grained wood on your floor, you should put down a "filler" before you stain or oil. This will close the pores in the wood and keep gallons of varnish from soaking into your boards. Your paint store can tell you about these.

Some of this sounds complicated, I know, but sanding a floor is a thrilling experience, so don't let me scare you off. And who knows, maybe your old place will have a floor in pretty decent shape and your job will be—well no, let's face it, it will never be *easy*.

FLOORCOVERINGS

In a kitchen or bathroom, you are likely to want a floor that is waterproof, greaseproof, and easy to clean. Instead of hiding the boards with something, you might want to sand, stain, and coat the wood with polyurethane varnish as in the example above. This is what we did in our kitchen and bathroom in Maine, and it worked out fine. You could also paint the floor and then polyurethane it. But if the boards are nondescript or in very bad shape, you will probably want to put some kind of cover over them.

The most common floorcoverings are vinyl, linoleum, and vinyl asbestos. Vinyl and linoleum come in both sheet and tile form. Vinyl asbestos comes only in tiles. It's too brittle to handle in sheets.

Sheet Goods/Vinyl and Linoleum

Tiles are much easier to work with than sheets. *Much* easier. Well, let's be honest, sheets are really a hassle. They come in 6 foot widths, and a 10 foot long piece of something like this is a lot heavier and more awkward to manage than you can probably imagine. With sheet goods you have to spread adhesive over an area 6 feet wide and who knows how long all at once, and keeping your shoes out of the stuff while trying to line up the cumbersome floorcovering is quite a trick. It can be done; Davene and I did two floors with sheet material. Okay, I did step in the paste a few times.

A nasty part of vinyl and linoleum is that you have to roll them with something, exerting a hundred pounds of pressure per square inch or something like that, it tells you on the can of adhesive, but it doesn't tell you how you're supposed to measure this. Rolling is hard work: I've used both a huge heavy wine bottle and a granite column and pressed with all my might and the floors stayed down, but for a few days afterward I stayed down too. It is also no fun to get your fingers caught under the roller—but every once in a while you'll do just that.

Most people seem to prefer vinyl to the other floorcoverings, I guess because it's the shiniest, has a "clear" look to its patterns, and doesn't need waxing (or so they say). But aside from being the most expensive covering, vinyl has a nasty habit of coming unstuck from the floor, so be warned. For this reason (as well as its lower cost), I'd use linoleum if I were going to mess with sheets. Once linoleum is down, it's down.

Vinyl Asbestos Tiles

As far as I'm concerned, vinyl asbestos tiles should be the amateur's choice. They are by far the easiest floorcovering to install (even fun), cheaper than linoleum and vinyl, and extremely durable. There's nothing wrong with them, except that most of them don't shine. (This horrendous fault can be overcome by a coat of wax—and there are some rather expensive vinyl asbestos tiles that do have a shiny finish.) They come in "service grade" ($\frac{1}{16}$" thick), or a $\frac{3}{32}$" thickness which will cost you more, hold up longer, and offer you some less offensive patterns. Vinyl asbestos tiles can be cut with ordinary scissors (linoleum and vinyl are quite thick, and you have to cut them with huge shears, a linoleum knife, or a utility knife), they conform to irregular surfaces, and you don't have to roll them. You just lay them in place and they stay down.

"Peel-and-stick"–type tiles are vinyl asbestos. Peel-and-sticks cost about twice as much as standard vinyl asbestos tiles. It's no job to buy the standard ones and put down adhesive yourself, so why spend the extra money?

One word of caution: vinyl asbestos tiles are very brittle, so handle the boxes carefully, open them carefully, take the tiles out gingerly, or you'll break off their corners. The warmer the tiles, the softer they are, so let the boxes stand at room temperature for a couple of hours before you open them.

Preparing Your Existing Floor for Tiles

You might get the impression from floor tile ads that you simply bring the tiles home and start slapping them down. You should be so lucky. Before you lay any floorcovering, you have to prepare your existing floor. If it's old warped boards (and it probably is), you should put down an underlayment. If you're putting in a new kitchen and bathroom and don't have any of the fixtures or cabinets in place yet, ⅜" particle board (see glossary) is a good choice. Nail the old floor down well into the joists, plane off any very high spots, and nail the particle board down with ringed underlayment nails. This will give you a firm, smooth base for your tiles. By the way, you can make a firm and good-looking floor with just particle board alone. Stained and given a coat of satin polyurethane, it has an unusual, attractive appearance and is inexpensive.

In a bathroom, after the underlayment is down, have the bathtub installed, then lay your tiles; this way you won't have to fit them around the sink and toilet. In the kitchen, install your base cabinets before you put the tiles down. You don't need a slick, expensive surface under cabinets.

If your bathroom already has fixtures in it, ⅜" particle board will be too thick and too difficult to work with. You can use ⅛" hardboard instead. Or, if the floorboards aren't in really bad shape, broken or cupped or with giant spaces between them, you can nail them down well, plane off any high spots, and paste 15 pound felt paper over them.

The felt comes in yard-wide rolls, and you get it at the floorcovering dealer's or at the lumberyard. The "15 pound" means that 100 square feet of the stuff (a "square") weighs 15 pounds. You stick this felt down with linoleum paste, and unfortunately you have to give it the roller treatment. Felt is most satisfactory underneath sheet linoleum, but I've had it work with vinyl asbestos tiles too. One nice thing about using felt: if you ever want to take the floorcovering up again, the felt will make the job a whole lot easier.

Instead of old boards, you might be faced with a worn out floorcovering in your bath or kitchen. On Lambert Street, the bathrooms had black marbleized asphalt tiles, not the most attractive and cheerful floor to our way of thinking. We pasted new vinyl asbestos tiles right over the old stuff and had no problems. However, the old floor was covered with a layer of wax about ⅛″ thick. We had to get that off or the new tiles wouldn't stick. We tried turpentine and alcohol and scrubbing with steel wool, but it was slow going. I finally went over the surface with the sanding attachment of my electric drill. This was fast and effective, though dusty. I was sanding asphalt tiles, so the dust wasn't terribly dangerous. I don't think I would've sanded vinyl asbestos tiles. Asbestos dust is extremely hazardous to your health.

There may be some spots where the floorboards or underlayment feel loose under the old floorcovering. Be sure to nail these down tightly with ringed nails.

Buying the Tiles

In or close to cities there are floorcovering discount houses that can save you quite a bit of money. Look especially for patterns that manufacturers have discontinued, or odd lots of tile the store happens to have on hand. There is some inevitable waste in any tiling job, and you will screw up some of the tiles, so buy extras. *America's Handyman Book* gives a tile waste allowance chart that will help you figure out how many tiles you will need. And most stores will figure this out for you if you give them the dimensions of your room.

Arranging the Tiles

Your floor is prepared, you have your tiles and you're eager to begin. You'll need: tile adhesive, paint thinner and rag (maybe), brush or roller, scissors, pencil, yardstick and steel square, clothes iron.

If you haven't removed the molding at the bottom of the baseboards, do it now. Then find the center point of one wall.

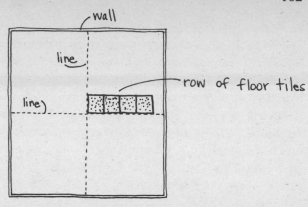

the tile plan as seen from above

From this point, draw a line across the floor to the center of the opposite wall. Now find the midpoint of this line. Put your steel square on the line at this spot and draw a line at right angles to the first. Extend this line until it touches the other two walls. (You have drawn a big cross on your floor.)

Start at the middle of the cross, and *without using any adhesive,* lay a row of tiles down next to each other until you reach one wall. Follow the same procedure in the other three directions. This will let you know how the tiles are going to look at the edge of the room. The idea is to avoid having a skinny (narrower than 2″) strip of tiles along any edge. Such strips of tiles not only look funny, they're also hard to cut and stick down. You also don't want the edge of any row of tiles to fall on a seam in the underlayment. The seam is likely to spread apart when the underlayment contracts, and give you a crack in your finished floor. If either of these conditions exist, move the appropriate line of your cross enough to take care of it.

Adhesive and Laying the Tiles

You know where the tiles will go, and you're ready to put down your adhesive. This used to be the awful part about vinyl asbestos tiles. The cement you used was a black sticky stuff that got all over you no matter how carefully you handled it. You had to spread it on the floor with a fine-tooth trowel, and you had to spread it *thin*. If you didn't, it would ooze up between the tiles literally forever. The stuff never dried, and you had yourself a permanent mess. They still sell this kind of adhesive. Don't buy it. There is a newer kind that you simply brush or roll on the floor; no trowel is needed. Ask for this kind at the store. It takes much less time to apply, and you don't have to worry about getting it on thin enough. It makes the job ten times easier than it used to be.

Make sure you get the right adhesive for the type of floorcovering you're using. Years ago, my father bought a whole bunch of vinyl asbestos tiles and put them down over the nice hardboard underlayment he'd installed. A few months later the underlayment began to contract, and the tiles cracked along every one of the underlayment's seams. The store guys had sold my father the wrong kind of cement. They were very sorry and gave him new cement and tiles, but what a job it was to fix that mess. You would think that in stores specializing in floorcoverings such mistakes would not be made, but—not long ago I was sold the wrong stuff too. Luckily I spotted the error before I put down the floor. Read the label on the can thoroughly before you use any adhesive. It will tell you what kinds of floorcovering you can use it with.

Your roll-on cement may still be dark and messy. If so, have a rag and some paint thinner handy for cleaning up mistakes. Brush or roll the adhesive over one block of the cross you've drawn, ¼ of the floor. (If the floor is huge, you may not want to do this much at once.) You have to paint along the edges of the cross carefully so as not to obscure the lines you've drawn. Once you get your first batch of tiles down, you won't have to worry about this any longer, as the tiles themselves will provide your guide.

Let the cement set up about 20 or 30 minutes until it no longer sticks to your finger when you push on it lightly. It will have a dull look to it at this point. Starting at the center of the cross and working toward one wall, lay down a row of full tiles. Take your time, the cement won't dry out too much. If the tiles seem very stiff, put them in a warm oven for a few minutes. This will soften them and make them flexible. Once your first row of tiles is down, lay another row beside it, then another, and so on until you've put down all the full tiles you can. Don't slide the tiles into place, just *lay* them down, or you may get adhesive coming up through the cracks after all. Spread adhesive over each of the other quarters of the floor and put down the rest of the full tiles. You can stand on the tiles right after they've been put in place; they won't slide around.

Once all the full tiles are down, measure the width of the partial tiles that fit against the wall, cut them and put them in place. Warm their undersides with the clothes iron before you cut, and the scissors will go through them easily. These tiles don't have to fit tightly against the wall because you are going to nail the baseboard shoe molding on top of them.

In spots where you do need a tight fit, up against the bathtub, for example, don't paste up the area where these partial tiles are to go. Take sheets of paper as wide as the tiles and line them up along the row of tiles that's been pasted down. Make sure the edge of each paper is snug against the edge of each tile. Smooth each paper out toward the tub, and with your fingernail, press the outline of the tub contour into it. Remove the paper and cut out the contour. Then lay the paper on a tile, trace around the contour with a pencil, soften the tile with your iron, and cut it to this shape. It should fit perfectly. (Make *sure* the pattern of the tile is running in the right direction before you cut it.) Cut all the tiles along the row this way, then brush on your paste, let it set, and put the tiles in place.

To fit around pipes, slit the tile with your scissors, then cut the hole for the pipe. It's a good idea to make a paper pattern for this kind of work too.

Once the whole floor is down, if any tiles don't lie completely flat, put a cloth on them, then let the iron sit on them a minute. This will soften them enough to put them in their place.

Laying Sheet Goods

Sheet goods are a lot more complicated, as you can imagine. You have to accurately cut one huge piece to fit around cabinets, pipes, etc. To get an accurate fit and paste up a large area and wrestle the sheet in place is no easy task. Don't try to do it alone. If a spot doesn't stick, you have to lift the whole piece up and squeeze more paste under it. No fun.

Painting Old Floorcoverings

People who take on old apartments sometimes paint the worn, dingy floorcovering in patterns and bright colors. But the paint will chip off fast if you aren't careful to get the old wax off, and the colors won't stay bright long unless you cover them with polyurethane varnish. Even with this, you can't count on the painted floor to hold up for very long. The difference in cost between painting the floor and tiling it with a less expensive grade of vinyl asbestos tile is slight. But of course you may not like the look of any of the less expensive vinyl asbestos tiles. I've often wondered why some flooring manufacturer doesn't put out a line of inexpensive vinyl rugs that have attractive and colorful designs on them instead of pink and black roses. I should think there'd be a market for them, but maybe I'm wrong.

CEMENTING A CELLAR FLOOR

A realtor and I were hunched down in the cellar of an abandoned row house. "Well yes," she said, looking sideways at me, "there isn't a whole lot of headroom, but fortunately the floor is dirt."

More fortunately, I thought, it could've been concrete, and two feet lower. She meant, of course, that since the floor was dirt, I could dig it out a couple of feet. If the floor had already been cemented, I would've had to live with it or else call in the jackhammers. Realtors can sell you the bright side of any catastrophe.

Now you don't just go digging a couple of feet of dirt out of your cellar without knowing what you're doing. That dirt may have a lot to do with supporting the foundation. If you are looking at a place with a very shallow cellar and you plan to increase the headroom, get someone to tell you exactly what it involves before you put down your money. Here's where the inspection service can come in handy again.

I've seen people who have done the whole thing: had the jackhammers in to chop up the old concrete, had the floor dug out, had the footings reinforced, had a new concrete floor put down. This costs plenty. I don't imagine it's very nice to live through, either. And it is definitely not a job for a do-it-yourselfer.

Now maybe your headroom's okay, but your floor is dirt. Dirt is, after all, dirty, and it really looks ridiculous with walnut paneling. It is also not a good base for water heaters, furnaces, pressure tanks, etc., and it tends to be damp. So you want to pour a concrete floor. Why not do it yourself? Before you rush to the phone and order the concrete, let me tell you about my experience.

Our Lambert Street basement had gone through a couple of transformations before we reached it. It seems that at one time whoever had the place decided to dig the floor deeper and put down concrete. Instead of getting rid of the dirt he dug up, he built a retaining wall in the back of the cellar and dumped all the dirt behind it.

The guy who owned the place right before we bought it

decided he wanted the floor still lower, so he had half the concrete jackhammered up again—and left it that way. This made it tough for the meter readers, and my hours at the workbench were less than a delight. I decided to put the concrete down again.

First I leveled the floor by hoeing and raking and filling in with spare dirt from my stash behind the retaining wall. Next I tamped the earth down firmly. The best way to do this is with an iron tamper designed for the purpose. If you can't rent one, throw a huge cellar party for fat people with big feet, and you might accomplish the same end.

Next I smashed up all the broken chunks of concrete with my 40 ounce hammer, making a gravel out of them. I then raked this gravel to a uniform depth across the floor. It is not essential to put a bed of gravel on a cellar floor. You can pour the concrete right over the dirt as long as the dirt's tamped down hard; this method was just the easiest way for me to get rid of the old concrete. (You do need gravel under sidewalks and other outdoor concrete projects; it gives you the drainage you need to keep freezing weather from cracking the concrete. Your cellar shouldn't freeze.)

There are two other often-recommended steps that I omitted. One is to cover the floor with plastic sheeting to moisture-proof it. The other is to lay down wire mesh for reinforcement. I didn't put down plastic because we had an exceptionally dry cellar floor. It is also a pain in the neck to get the plastic to stay where you want it when you're working with the concrete and to keep from punching holes in it. (I've had some experience with it since.) I didn't use the mesh partly because of the added trouble and expense, and partly because if I ever wanted to chop a hole in that floor for any reason, I would've had an unbelievable time. I also figured that 3″ of concrete was going to be pretty strong on its own.

I found a Saturday when my friend John and my brother-in-law Bob were free, and ordered the concrete in advance. If you're doing a big job like this and you live in the city, by all means buy your concrete already mixed. In the country you might try mixing it yourself if you can get hold of a power mixer. (You might even try a manual mixer if you need some exercise; mixing concrete by hand is hard and heavy work, but some people, like Scott Nearing, swear by it.) Hand mixing in the city is impractical. It means a big mound of sand on your sidewalk, and the kids on the block will have half of it down the sewer by sunset.

Before you call the concrete company, make sure you know how much of the stuff you need. (You'll want your floor to be 3 to 4 inches thick.) It's sold by the cubic yard, and 1 cubic yard is usually the minimum they'll deliver. One cubic yard, by the way, is a lot of concrete. (A 90 pound bag of ready-mix yields about ⅔ of a cubic *foot.*)

Another warning: You and your friends may be unfortunate enough to have steady work, and, like me, you may have to do the job on a Saturday. The cement place may charge you extra because Saturday is not a regular working day. Make sure you arrange a definite time for delivery when you order, or they may pull this one on you later: "You the guy that wants the concrete? Well look, it's 10 of 12, and if we go past 12 o'clock it's overtime and we get $5 a minute for overtime, so we're gonna hafta get that stuff down there kinda fast, or else . . ." That's the one they pulled on me.

It didn't much matter, because I didn't have any wheelbarrows anyway. You see, you should have some wheelbarrows so you can move the stuff around to the remote corners of the area you're working on fairly easily. (Nothing about this job goes *really* easily.) I didn't have any wheelbarrows, so they just stuck the chute in the window and made a concrete mountain against the cellar wall.

I'd been in some jams with old houses before, but this situation looked hopeless. John, who'd had experience with concrete work, snapped me out of my daze with, "Let's go, it's

gonna set up!" and a furious burst of shoveling. The three of us
spent the next half hour in Coronary City. We shoveled and
raked and hoed that stuff across the floor non-stop, and if you
think snow shoveling takes something out of you, try this. There
is no staying out of the mess either, so wear galoshes. Bob's
concreted tennis shoes were still sitting in the cellar when we
sold the house, a monument to I'm not sure what.

The books always have you level-off concrete by jiggling the
edge of a long heavy board back and forth across its surface. I
had an old 2 x 6 around and actually entertained a foolish
thought of doing this. But there was no place to stand while we
jiggled, other than in the concrete. So we put down small pieces
of plywood instead, kneeled on them and troweled the whole
thing level, working our way toward the cellar steps. (The
plywood distributes your weight enough to keep you from
sinking.) You want to trowel enough to level and smooth things
out, but you don't keep going over and over any one spot or the
finished surface is likely to be dusty forever.

After the troweling was done, John went over the surface with
a push broom, giving the floor a uniform, non-skid texture. The
whole job took just about two hours, which I didn't think was
too bad. The experience had a profound effect on John.
"Whenever things look really bad," he told me a short while
back, "I think about that cellar floor. And I realize that anything
is possible, absolutely *anything*."

Sound like fun? Passed your latest stress cardiogram? Then go
to it!

9 PAINTING AND PASTING THINGS TOGETHER, FROM WALLS TO TRIM TO ROOF

PRACTICALLY EVERYONE WHO TACKLES A WRECK OF A HOUSE or an old apartment expects to do his own painting and is pretty sure he can handle it. So I won't have much to say about painting as such—but I do have some comments on things related to it.

PREPARING THE SURFACE, THE AMATEUR'S PITFALL

Most non-allergic people find painting enjoyable. Boring after a while, yes, but perhaps even soothing in its very boredom. It's not strenuous either physically or mentally, and your mind is free to run all over the place while you work. Painting is highly gratifying, too: nothing else works such magic with so little effort.

You can often get friends to give you a hand with your

painting. But just try to get help preparing your beat-up surfaces. Just about no one enjoys preparing the surface to be painted, and that's why it's so often slighted. But without good surface preparation, that paint job isn't going to look very nice and it isn't going to last. If you have a house (or an apartment) you think you'll be staying in for a while, you want the job to last.

Removing Wallpaper

Maybe the wallpapered walls in your old place are in good shape: the paper is smooth, just a couple of layers thick, and stuck on tight. Whenever you take off paper you'll find trouble, so you may want to paint or paper over these good walls and save the headaches for the far-off future. But let's be realistic: The paper in most old places is layers and layers thick, halfway peeled off, stained, split, and bulging. And there is nothing to do but get rid of it—completely. This will reveal a thousand cracks, holes, lumps, the place where the fireplace used to be, etc. But it's best to deal with these tragedies right at the start, rather than try to cover them up and then have them pop through your paint job two months after you've cleaned your last brush.

Removing the wallpaper is one of the first jobs you should do on your old house. It lets you know how bad off your walls are, is a nice mess to get out of the way early, and lets you put a brightening coat of latex on the place.

If you want to, you can rent a steamer from your paint store. These things spray hot water vapor through little holes in a flat wide gadget you hold in your hand. They're supposed to work like a charm. I don't like them. First, they don't work like a charm, at least not the ones I've used. They work very slowly. Second, they eat electricity. And third, they are not fun to work with on hot humid days or if you wear glasses. I prefer a bucket of hot water with a package of wallpaper remover added to it. Slop the water on liberally with a large paint brush, a scrub brush or a wallpaper paste brush if you have one. As soon as a section starts to look a little dry, slop it up again. Do it a third time, and while it's good and wet, go at it with your scraper. Don't use a putty-knife-type scraper, get the kind with the foot-long handle and sharp, stiff, razor-like blade. It will make your job much easier. Your paint store should carry it.

There may be a few spots that even with repeated soaking and scraping simply won't come off. You will just have to let them dry, then sand down their edges with fine sandpaper. After a couple of coats of paint, they should be undetectable. Once you've gotten off all the paper you can, brush the walls down with a push broom or dustbrush and put on the coat of white latex.

Suppose the paper has been painted over. Professionals can get it off, but you will find it mighty tough going. If you're really determined to remove it, rough up the painted surface with coarse sandpaper, then apply the remover. But your best bet is to scrape off any loose or bulging spots and let the rest alone. Sand the edges of the scraped areas with fine sandpaper. If they are especially high or rough, you can treat them as you would chipped areas. (I'll get to that in a second.)

If you have a plasterboard wall with wallpaper on it, you have to remove the paper very, very carefully. This is one time the steamer comes in handy; it can sometimes soften the paste under the paper just enough to let you lift up a corner and peel the stuff off. It's a trick not to gouge a plasterboard wall with a scraper. And don't slop buckets of water on plasterboard—it'll fall apart.

Peeling, Chipping, Dents

Earlier I discussed the repair of large breaks and cracks in plaster walls. You'll also be faced with lots of little dents and gouges. These can be conquered with ready mixed vinyl spackle and a putty knife. You'll have an easier time if you've sealed the wall with latex; this will get rid of the grit that will otherwise mix with your spackle and interfere with smoothing and adhesion.

Often you'll find old walls with thick and brittle paint that's peeling and chipping like mad. Scrape all this loose paint off and roll on your coat of white latex. Then use vinyl spackle to cover the edges of the areas you've scraped. Spread it well over the chipped part with your 3″ putty knife and smooth it out. This will not only make the edges of the scars disappear, blending them in with the old paint that's still okay, it will glue them to the wall. This is very important. If you don't glue these edges down, a year or two after you put on your finish coat of paint they will curl up and start to flake off again, and you'll have to do the job over.

Calcimine

Maybe (oh, lucky you!) you have calcimine on your walls. This stuff was used years ago, before the easy-to-work-with indoor paints were formulated. It has a hard, glossy, chalk-like look to it. If you wet it, its colors will run. When you find stuff like this on your walls, fall on your knees and gnash your teeth, then get a bucket of warm water and detergent, a scrub brush and some rags, and get busy. I'm sorry, but you'll just have to do it, paints won't stick to this stuff. Even if they did it would bleed right through them.

Bleeding

You have the walls cleaned, painted with a coat of medium-priced white latex, and you've patched all the holes and nicks and gouges. Now you'll see that some stains have bled through the latex paint. Old wallpaper may make rust-colored marks, old water stains may too, old crayon, paint, dye, blood, old god-only-knows will all leave their own special signatures on your plaster. You can put a dozen coats of latex on these spots and you'll be lucky if the stains don't come through every coat. To stop the bleeding, at least in most cases, you'll need shellac. You can use regular "white" shellac (which is clear), or, especially if you have a large area you want to seal, you can use a white primer with a shellac base. There are a number of these on the market. Sears sells one, and one of the best known is B-I-N.

If you anticipate a lot of staining and want to play safe, you can use this shellac-based primer to begin with instead of the white latex. It does a very good job of sealing the surface so that subsequent coats of paint will dry with a uniform finish. It dries in 45 minutes or so, and as soon as it does, you can paint over it. Its major drawback is that unlike most paints it is very thin, and it's easy to splash it all over the place. When working with it on ceilings, it's a good idea to wear goggles or you might get the primer in your eyes, as Davene did. To clean your brushes you will need denatured alcohol or household ammonia and warm water, not paint thinner or mineral spirits.

Don't keep shellac or shellac-based primer around for more than a few months after you've opened it, because it loses its drying powers rapidly. And if you use a shellac that won't dry, you have got yourself a mess. We know. We used old varnish around the edge of the kitchen floor in our old apartment. Guck. The roaches never made it to the table in that place.

Now, if you use a latex paint over the shellac, it may bring out the stain again. Then you have to coat it with more shellac. Doing this a couple of times will usually kill it. But if you have a large stained area, an entire wall, for instance, consider using an oil- or alkyd-based finish paint instead of a latex. It will be much harder for the stain to fight its way through that.

On Lawrence Street our hallways had a maroon fiber wainscoating that had been badly ruined by dampness on the second floor. We scraped the damaged part away and were faced with a pockmarked wall with huge maroon streaks running through it. We decided to texture paint the wall, but first we rolled a coat of oil-based primer over it to kill the stains. It seemed to work:

when the primer dried, you could barely see some pale maroon in a couple of spots. We applied the texture paint, a latex: zip, all the stains came to life again. We then painted over the texture paint with an alkyd-based flat white—and the stains disappeared again. For the heck of it, I painted a little section of this finished wall with flat white latex—and sure enough, the stains came back. The water soluble paints will pull stains right through your primer, so when in doubt, use oil or alkyd.

Texture Paints

Earlier I described our use of a powdered texture paint which was less a paint than a plaster. (See "Soft Spots" in Chapter Five.) The thinner, latex texture paints that come ready mixed are also quite useful and can save you an awful lot of time repairing your walls and ceilings.

Peter and Jack had an old bathroom that they wanted to make look decent fast. The bottom half of the room had been tiled and was okay. The top half was painted plaster—crumbling, cracking and full of scars. Jack went to buy some latex texture paint while Peter and I did the finish patching. Jack came back from the store looking doubtful: "When I told the guy I was going to use this in a bathroom, he just shook his head and said, 'Uh-uh.' " I told him not to worry. (This always comes easily to me when I'm working on someone else's house.) The three of us slapped the texture paint on in heavy swirls, covering every crack, hole and gouge. I explained that it would dry to a dull and somewhat porous finish, and that the man in the store was probably worried about how the moisture of bathing, etc. would affect it. I assured them that it was no problem.

The next day, when the texture paint was completely dry, we painted over the whole thing with an alkyd-based semi-gloss enamel. That was nine years ago. Today there are a few cracks in the surface of the paint and a piece of plaster near the mirror is loose. I don't think that's bad, all things considered.

It's hard to get a decent finish with latex texture paint

alone—its surface is dull and uneven when dry, and you'll probably want to use it as a base coat and cover it with something else. If you haven't primed the wall you want to texture, don't. The texture paint will bond firmly to the raw plaster, and the primer will do more good over it than under it.

Some people are dead set against texture paints, they just can't stand the look of them. (Of course, they can have many looks according to the way you apply them.) Even if you don't especially like them, consider using them in hallways or other out-of-the-way areas, or in an old apartment with pockmarked or crumbly plaster. They will save you an incredible amount of patching and sanding of minor defects.

Sand texture paint is especially good for this. The texture is barely noticeable, but it hides very well; the grains of sand really fool your eye and all sorts of imperfections disappear. The paint is easy to apply with a roller, but be sure to wear a long-sleeved shirt, because otherwise your arms will get covered with it.

On Lawrence Street all our wallpaper came off okay except for the paper on the dining room ceiling. Scraping ceilings is torture and we soon quit, they must've welded the stuff on. We covered it with white sand paint and it looked terrific.

Texture paints do have a couple of drawbacks. Once you've textured your walls you're stuck with them that way; it will be next to impossible to untexture them. And if the texture is pronounced, it will gather dust. The sand paint will pick up dust too. The thing I dislike about it, though, is that if you rub into a wall covered with it you get, well—sanded. It can take the skin right off. That's why it's best on ceilings.

OLD WOODWORK

As bad as your walls are, your woodwork is likely to be worse. Dented, chipped, lumpy, it presents a formidable challenge. If it's not in too bad shape, you might just want to scrape off any loose paint, sand the marred spots, wash with Spic and Span to get off any dirt and grease, and repaint. But if it's badly beat up, you'll want to remove the old finish and get down to the wood again.

This may seem drastic, but it's the only way you'll get a nice job. Also, you shouldn't try to sand large amounts of woodwork smooth, you'll run yourself into the ground. I know. I've done it.

Paint Removing

You soften the old paint with a chemical paint remover or heat. If you use a paint remover, the paste-type, water-soluble kind is the most practical. Paint removers are messy and dangerous. Always wear gloves while using them; it's not a bad idea to wear goggles, too. Don't splash them around, they taste terrible. Be sure to let them sit on the paint long enough to soften it. If you're impatient you'll waste time, money, and energy. Often you will have to use two or three (or even more!) applications to get all the old finish off.

Once the paint is soft, remove it with a stiff putty knife, scrapers, and coarse steel wool. There are all kinds of scrapers; some have triangular, some have rectangular, some have rounded heads. It's good to have a few kinds on hand, because you'll run into all sorts of odd curves and angles.

Instead of paint remover, you might try a propane torch. It's quicker, cleaner, and more fun. You can't use one to take the paint off things you're going to put a clear finish on, though. The flame will scorch the wood, and you'll never get those black marks off.

The bad thing about a torch, of course, is the possibility of burning the place down. This possibility is very real. Torches are *very* hot, and old dry wood is easy to ignite. You shouldn't use a torch near wood shingles or siding. But inside the house you're on pretty safe ground if you stay alert, have water handy, and keep a fire extinguisher in reserve.

I'm making it sound worse than it is. I've never had a fire in all the years I've used a torch. I think most fires start because you forget to pay attention to what's going on. The steady roar of the flame hypnotizes you, it's just so fascinating. And suddenly you realize you're burning.

To light the propane torch, strike your match, hold it right next to the tip of the torch and turn the gas on very slowly. This way the gas won't blow your match out. Professionals use a flint starter, so they don't run into this problem. (They cost less than a dollar, so consider buying one.) Once the flame is lit, turn the gas up high enough to do the job.

Just heat the paint to the point where it turns soft and scrapeable, then take the torch away. Watch out where you set it down. Keep the flame well back from anything combustible, including yourself.

There are electric paint softeners available at paint stores if this torch thing sounds too dangerous.

After you've removed the paint with either chemicals or heat, you'll have to do some sanding with a medium or fine paper to get things really smooth. Try to sand as little as possible, but get off anything obvious. Fill any holes or dents with vinyl spackle. Coat the woodwork with a heavy-bodied alkyd-based primer, the best you can buy. These primers cover all sorts of small defects and provide an excellent base for finish paint. Don't thin them.

It's best to use an alkyd finish coat, too. Latex semi-gloss paints give an attractive, hard, washable finish that's fine for walls, especially kitchens and bathrooms—but they chip off of woodwork. All you have to do is bang into them with something, and good-bye.

Repairing Broken Trim

Sometimes you'll come across a piece of window trim or baseboard that's had a chunk knocked out of it. You can usually repair the damage with water putty or linseed oil putty. Stick it on the broken spot and mold it to the shape of the surrounding trim. A little sanding and some paint and you'll scarcely see it. This is an especially handy method to use on curved sections of molding. Today's baseboards never curve, but in the old days people had the time, patience, and desire to make such things. It's usually these curves that get zonked each time the furniture is moved, and eventually they crack and fall away. Did you ever try to curve a piece of molding? Take my word for it, it's far easier to repair the damage with putty.

Replacing Trim

You might decide that you want to pry off straight pieces of badly damaged trim and replace them. Well, simply take a bit of the molding to the lumberyard and have them match it. Oh sure.

Once I built a new wall and wanted the new baseboard molding to match what I had on the other walls. The design of the existing molding was an extremely common one. I took a scrap piece to the lumberyard and asked the man for something similar. Did we ever have a chuckle. The modern equivalent to what I had was just a little more than half as thick as the old stuff. Since I was using the molding on a new wall and was more concerned with design than thickness, I bought some of the new material, clung to it tightly so it wouldn't blow away, and left a wiser man. If I'd needed an exact match, I would've had to go to a lumberyard where they do millwork and have them make it up special for me. This is not cheap, as you can imagine, but sometimes it's all you can do.

OUTSIDE TRIM

No matter how much the inside trim is neglected, at least it's away from the sun, wind, and rain. The elements can beat the devil out of exposed wood. The outside of your old window frame may look pretty hopeless. If it's full of rot, it *is* hopeless and you'll have to replace it. But most old trim comes back to life surprisingly well, even if it's rotted some, is cracked, pitted, porous, and loose.

None of our houses had seen any outside paint in at least fifteen years. Our Lawrence Street frames and sills turned out fairly nicely, but it took us till Lambert Street to learn how to restore outside trim really well.

Mr. Nesbitt's Magic Formula

We learned from Mr. Nesbitt, an old painter who came through the neighborhood every spring looking for work. We were pressed for time and agreed to have him paint the trim on the front of the house. I had already scraped the paint off the third floor window frames and had applied a thinned primer to one of them. Thinned because I wanted it to soak into the dried-out wood. Mr. Nesbitt surveyed my work with chagrin.

"No, no," he said, "you can't do the job like that. You can't just put that primer on like that, it won't stick. That old wood is dry as a bone, all the life's gone out of it, there's *nothin'* gonna stick to that. Now of course once wood is dead, you can't put the life back in, but there is somethin' you *can* do. I'll do it on your front, and listen, get a piece of paper and write this down, you can do it on the rest of the house when you get around to it." He then dictated this formula:

"You take two parts boiled linseed oil—now that's *boiled*, not raw—you got that? And one part turpentine, *not* mineral spirits. Put that in a bottle and shake it up good. Get a good thick brush and slap this onto them dried-out sills and frames and watch them drink it up. After all them years in the sun they are *thirsty*. Goose 'em up again and let 'em dry a day or two. Then do it all over again, goose it up real good with that brush and this time it won't soak up so much. If it looks like it's still thirsty, wait another day and do it again. When you're done and it's all dried out it should be a little shiny and not sticky, and you're all set."

This really works. If there's any old paint left on the trim, burn it off before you begin. Once this linseed formula has dried, cover the whole frame and sill with two coats of good exterior primer. Thin the first coat a little. Be sure to use an *exterior* primer.

Incidental information: In Philadelphia I bought a lot of paint at a little store on east Market Street. The owner had suffered a stroke and his speech was badly slurred. One time I asked him for an interior primer. He sniffed and wheezed and shuffled around and plopped an exterior primer on the counter. I pointed out his error. He roared something unintelligible by way of explanation and I stood there looking blank. He repeated the thing, apparently some sort of aphorism, two more times. I was getting that red panicked feeling when the man's wife rushed to the rescue. "He said," she translated, "you can use the outside inside, but you can't use the inside outside." "Oh," I said, handing her a ten, "that's what I thought he said," and I took the exterior primer home and used it inside.

I suppose the man's saying is true, especially now that paints don't have lead in them anymore: you can use an exterior primer inside the house, but you can't use an interior primer outside—it won't hold up. But you're almost sure to pay more for the exterior primer, so why use it where you don't have to?

Paint Brushes

I never buy good paint brushes. I don't buy cheap ones, but I don't get Chinese bristle, either. Because sooner or later I'll put a paint-loaded brush in a plastic bag instead of going to the trouble of cleaning it—just overnight, you understand, no sense cleaning it when I'm going to use it the next day—and then I'll forget about it for a week. Do this a couple of times and your brush is done for. When it's nylon bristle it's not too painful, but when it's good stuff, it smarts.

Paint as a Stain

Remember that any oil or alkyd paint can be thinned with turpentine to make a stain. You can get some interesting effects this way.

Pitted Window Sills

After years of neglect, your windowsills may be deeply pitted and grooved. Painting over these grooves is pretty futile: rain will collect in them and the paint will soon start coming off again. For a really permanent repair of such a sill, first soak it with Mr. Nesbitt's linseed oil and turpentine formula, then fill the grooves with wood filler or water putty. Let the sill dry thoroughly, then prime it. After the primer dries, paint it with a coat of liquid epoxy glue. This will give you a hard, smooth, and durable surface.

If you have only one or two sills in bad condition, you can buy your epoxy at an auto supply or hardware store. If you have a number of sills to do, buy larger quantities at a marine supply or from a company that makes the stuff. Sears also carries it in gallon sizes. Never buy it in little tubes for jobs like this, it'll cost too much.

For an extra durable sill repair, use two coats of epoxy with a layer of fiberglass cloth between them. This cloth is a smooth, loosely woven mesh of fiberglass threads. It is often used to fix holes in cars, and you can buy it at auto supply stores.

The fiberglass cloth and epoxy method is an excellent way to patch holes in your gutters and downspouts. You can also use it to bridge a rotten spot between two areas that are sound. Let's say, for instance, that your window frame is rotted where it

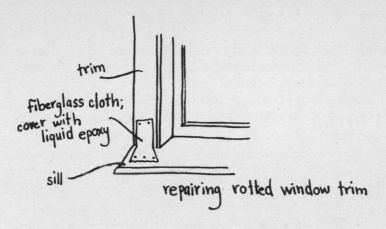

trim

fiberglass cloth; cover with liquid epoxy

sill

repairing rotted window trim

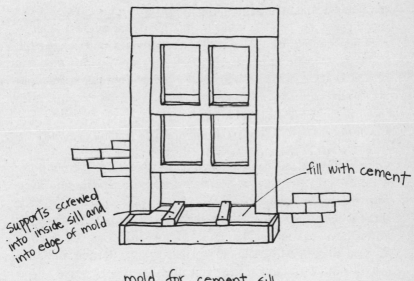

fill with cement

supports screwed into inside sill and into edge of mold

mold for cement sill

meets the sill. Make sure the rotted area is dry, then soak it with epoxy. Above the rotted spot, tack a piece of fiberglass cloth onto the window frame. Run the cloth down over the rotted spot, pressing it into the epoxy, and tack it to the sill. Coat it with epoxy. This will seal and bond the sill and frame and keep it serviceable for years.

What about really rotten sills? In a frame house, you have to take the old sill out and put in a new one. Taking out the old sill is the hardest part of this. Saw it in half, then pry up each side with a pry bar. Replacement is simply a piece of wood cut to the right size.

In a brick house you don't have to remove the whole sill if it isn't too far gone. You can replace the rotted area with cement. Scrape away the rotted part. Build a mold out of wood to hold the cement and nail it temporarily to the window frame. (The mold looks a lot like a window box.) Drive a whole bunch of galvanized common nails into the remaining sound windowsill. Fill the form with sand mix. When it's set, remove the form. The cement will be held in place by the protruding nail heads, and you'll have yourself a durable sill.

Caulking

Once your trim has been patched and primed, caulk around the window frame to prevent drafts and leaks. You may find deep gaps where the window frame meets the wall. You want to stuff these cracks to about $\frac{1}{4}''$ from the surface before you caulk, or you'll have to buy caulk by the truckload. You are usually advised to stuff with oakum, a rather greasy, fibrous rope that you buy by the pound at the paint store or building supply. You can buy top of the round for about the same price. You can use steel wool instead, but strands of it will stick out of the cracks and foul up your caulk. The best thing I've found for the job is fiberglass insulation. It's cheap, it insulates, it packs tightly.

What kind of caulking compound should you use? There are

many varieties on the market. I prefer one of the most expensive, butyl rubber marine caulk. It costs five or six times more than the cheapest caulk you can buy. But the cheapest caulk will most likely begin to crack and pull away in a couple of years. The rubber should be good for ten years or more. Be sure to use enough to bridge the gap between the window frame and the wall because air and water can find the tiniest opening. (If you have plastic lenses in your glasses, watch that you don't get this stuff on them; I don't know how you get it off.)

Rope caulk, the stuff that comes in rolls, is handy for places where it's hard to maneuver your caulking gun, but it won't stick as well as the cartridge kind.

ROOF REPAIRS—NOT FOR THOSE WITH VERTIGO

And I'm not kidding. I had vertigo off and on for eight months once, and it was all I could do to keep from falling off the front step. If you feel queasy up high, or if your roof is pitched, it's best to stay off it and leave the repairs to professionals.

I hate making this recommendation, because roofers are the repairmen I trust the least. The ones I've met have always looked for the easiest and quickest way to do the job—whether or not this way would stop the leak. So shop for a roofer carefully. And never pay one until you've had a chance to see if his job has done you any good.

Finding the leak is half the battle in roof repair. If you can trace the water's source before the roofers come, you'll have a fighting chance of getting the job done right. I know it's the roofer's duty to find the leak, but he's in a terrible rush, so instead of getting down on his hands and knees and poking around, he'll just slap pitch over your whole darn roof and disappear.

If your roof sheathing boards are exposed in the attic, you can probably find the leak from inside the house. Wait until the ceiling starts to drip, or squirt a powerful blast from your hose in the suspicious area, then search the sheathing for the hole. It is often some distance from the place where the water shows up in the house. Once you find it, circle it with chalk and stick a piece of wire through it so you can locate it up on the roof.

Maybe you have a roof that's flat or gently pitched. Okay then, try to do the job yourself. (But if the roof is tile or slate, you'd better not mess with it. You'd probably only break things up by walking on it, and it's doubtful if you'd be able to cure the problem anyway.)

Most city roofs are metal or built-up. If you have a metal roof in good condition, rejoice. They are tremendous things that last for years and years. You renew the worn surface of a metal roof by brushing asphalt coating over it. This stuff will often seal pinhole leaks. If you don't have any leaks, it will prevent them by protecting the metal from rust. So if that metal roof looks threadbare, slop it up. I've read that metal roofs should be coated every five years, but our Lawrence Street roof hadn't been done in thirty, and it only leaked where a fallen chimney brick had punctured it.

You apply the coating with a roofing brush, which looks like a flat push broom with stiff bristles. It costs about $2 (exclusive of handle). You'll need to have paint thinner and some rags on hand because roof coating is awful stuff. It's absolutely impossible to stay out of it. You will get it on your hands, shirt, shoes, eyelids, even your tongue if you talk to yourself. Believe me, no matter how careful you are, you'll get it on something. Take your shoes off before you go back into the house.

One kind of roof coating has sunlight-reflecting aluminum flakes in it. It costs about three times as much as the regular plain black stuff, but it's worth it to keep your attic or third floor cooler in those sizzling city summers.

Built-up roofs consist of layers of tar and felt. The tar is applied hot, and a first class renewal job means another coating with hot stuff. This is not something that you do yourself. But you can give a built-up roof the same coating treatment as a metal roof, then scatter sand across it to help protect the surface. This will give you some time to save up the money for the hot roof which you will someday need.

What about the hole in the roof? If you can see the hole but can't get your hands on it due to fear of death, you might be able to take a piece of wood lath, smear some plastic roof cement (more horrible black stuff) on it, and reach the hole with it. Or you could try the long caulking gun method that I mentioned in the Introduction. You just might be lucky enough to have it work.

But expansion and contraction often open holes up again. So if you can reach the leak, it's better to bridge it with something for a really good seal.

Here's how to proceed: First, trowel a layer of plastic roof cement over the leaking area. Spread the cement several inches beyond the edges of the hole. Now most books tell you to put down a layer of aluminum foil or roofing felt, press it down tightly, then cover this with another layer of roof cement. I've found this doesn't hold up too well: the edges of the felt or foil can curl.

Instead, paint the cemented patch with roof *coating*. Then lay a square of heavy cloth (like canvas) on top of the wet coating, and press it down well with your stiff roofing brush. Coat the top of the canvas liberally with more roof coating. Then lay down another slightly larger piece of canvas, press it down, coat it, and cover with still another piece of canvas. Make each square of canvas a couple of inches bigger than the preceding one. Stick the edges of the last piece of canvas down with roof *cement*. Put the cement both under and on top of the edges, then slop a bunch of coating over all this. This should hold up nicely. And make you look like the tar baby.

In the country, the most common roof you'll run into is

asphalt shingle. This kind of roof has a pitch, but maybe you can reach the leaking spot from a ladder. If a lot of the granular coating is worn off the shingles or their edges are curled up, you'll have to think about a new roof. But in the meantime, you can take care of holes.

Hit them with roof cement. For extra protection, coat them (and any spots where the granules have worn off) with roof coating. You might try the kind that's reinforced with fiberglass threads. This stuff has a consistency between regular roof coating and roof cement. It costs about three times as much as regular roof coating. You'll need a stiff brush to apply it (but not necessarily a roofing brush). I am a little hesitant in recommending it because although it looks like good stuff and it's worked for me, I haven't had it on my roof long enough to tell if it's worth the extra money.

10 YOUR PLUMBING

MOST CITIES WON'T LET YOU DO MUCH PLUMBING. NEITHER
will a lot of rural areas. Plumbing codes are tough. They have to
be. If you screw up the plumbing, you and others can get mighty
sick.

There are some simple plumbing problems, however, that
anyone can fix, and you definitely want to fix them: plumbers
cost almost as much as dentists. There are times when you'll
need them, but there's no point in paying them to do the small
stuff. Before you buy an old house, get hold of some library
books and find out how a plumbing system works and what it
consists of. Plumbing is vulnerable in many ways, and you're
bound to run into some problems.

PIPES

If you're buying a city house that's been vacant for any length of
time—say three days—you will need lots of plumbing work.

Nothing disappears from an empty house as fast as copper pipe. And there is nothing kids enjoy smashing more than a toilet. If the house had brass pipe, it has undoubtedly vanished too. If it had galvanized iron, it's still there, but forget it, you'll have to replace it. Our Lawrence Street house had galvanized pipe all over the place. The first time we turned on the water the whole house got a shower, there were that many pinholes in the stuff. It was a great sprinkler system.

The Soil Stack

You may find a tub or a sink you can salvage. That's fine. But the thing you really hope to find intact is the soil stack, the waste pipe into which all the sinks, tubs, and toilets drain. If it's cast iron, chances are no one will have messed with it, and if it isn't broken, count your blessings. You will definitely want to plan your new bathroom and kitchen around it. The soil stack is a big expense in a plumbing installation. We had a section of cast iron stack installed from the basement to the second floor on Lawrence Street. Even back then it cost $600, and that was considered cheap.

Maybe after you've bought the place the cast iron stack that looked okay turns out to have a leak at a joint. Okay, you've got a job for the plumber to do.

Sometimes the pipe itself will have a crack in it. Now, this is a job the plumber will *want* to do, because he gets paid a truckload every time he wrestles with cast iron, but I wouldn't let him do it. On Lawrence Street, the part of the stack that we didn't replace ran from one end of the cellar to the other. It was cracked near the point where it went through the wall. Every time we drained the sink or flushed the toilet, drip, drip, drip on the cellar floor. It would've cost us a couple of hundred dollars to have the plumbers sweat and grunt and curse. I fixed it myself with no grunts, no sweat, and only a couple of curses. First I put a ban on all sink and toilet use, dried the area around the leak with my torch, then coated it all with paste epoxy putty. I wrapped strips of heavy cloth around this, more epoxy, more cloth, etc., finishing with a coat of epoxy. In six years, the pipe never leaked. If I had the job to do over, I'd use fiberglass cloth and liquid epoxy, and I'm sure it would last forever.

WATER PRESSURE

One thing you'd like to check out before you buy an old place is the water pressure, but you probably won't be able to. If a city house has been standing vacant a while, the water has been turned off out at the street. There's a valve down under one of those square metal boxes on the sidewalk. Way down. You have to turn it on with a "key" several feet long, and the water company has those.

If the pressure is poor when you turn the old plumbing on, it could be corrosion in old galvanized pipes or too small pipes in the cellar. It could be just one piece of gunked-up pipe that's slowing things down. Or it could be that the pipe that runs from the water main itself into the house is corroded. This pipe is several feet under the sidewalk, and it will cost a couple of hundred dollars to have it dug up and replaced. It is possible that the pressure from the main is poor. This is most likely if you're some distance from the main. If the neighbors have good pressure and you don't, you know this isn't the problem.

In a house out in the country, the system has been drained and the water's in the well. When a pump gets constant use it will last for years, but it doesn't take a long idle period to wreck it. A few years of disuse and it may be rusted solid; the motor will work, but that's about all. Poor pressure in a well system can be due to any number of things, but you won't discover what they are until you've already shelled out your money for the house, so cross your fingers.

OLD FIXTURES

The old fixture you'll probably think of getting rid of is the toilet, but chances are this is the one you can keep. If the thing doesn't flush, don't toss it out unless the tank or bowl are broken. Clean it up, replace its damaged parts, put on a new seat and it'll be good as ever.

The toilet may be the old "washdown" kind. How can you tell? The hole where the water disappears is at the front of the bowl instead of at the back. Also, the bowl bulges or has a long ridge on its outside front. These old toilets are supposed to clog more easily than the newer kinds, and they don't block the gases from the sewer as well as toilets of newer design. (I shouldn't really call them "old"; a friend had one installed in his house less than ten years ago.) Sewer gas is not supposed to be healthy for you, but then neither are cities. We've lived with washdown toilets and we're still here, and if I had a washdown today in good condition, I'd keep it.

You may want to hang on to your charming old sinks and bathtub, but here you may have problems. The faucets are probably shot. And the porcelain surface is worn to the point where it holds all the grime. If not, you're really in luck.

We've done it both ways: we've kept the fixtures and we've bought new ones. If the old ones are in good shape it would be foolish to get rid of them. What about buying or scrounging old fixtures? That's a different matter. If it's something special, okay. On Lawrence Street we were given a marble-topped sink with a china bowl and a hand-carved mahogany cabinet. Fine, you don't run across this kind of thing every day. We got a good deal on a kitchen sink, and that was also fine. We were also given a big old eagle claw cast iron bathtub. Not so fine, as we'll see in a minute.

Another thing: If your house already has old fixtures, the plumber will run new lines to them, no problem. But if you go out and scrounge old fixtures for him to hook up, he will probably not like you—because he loses his markup on the brand-new fixtures he would've sold you, which is not inconsiderable. And he may try to make up his "loss" in his installation price.

Turning Off the Water

Before you take any plumbing apart, you have to turn off the water at a point below the spot where you're working. In the ideal house, you'll have shut-off valves below every sink, tub, and toilet. (Shut-off valves for the tub and shower are usually inside a little door on the wall behind the fixtures.) But you will not be living in the ideal house unless you have had all new fixtures put in or new lines run and have told the plumber you want these valves. Some plumbers will put them in as a matter of course and some won't, so be sure to check—you definitely want them.

In your old place you'll probably have some fixtures with shut-off handles and some without. On Lambert, we had valves for every line or fixture except the first floor bathroom sink; somehow it got lost in the shuffle. In order to work on that sink we had to shut off the water to the entire house. Sometimes you'll find a valve in the cellar that will turn off the water to one floor; just check the pipes and see if they have any handles in the middle of them. In other cases you will have to shut off the whole works. Find the place where the water line comes into the house; shortly after this point, you'll see a handle. Turn it and your water is off.

Old Toilets

Most old toilets are pretty much the same inside. They look something like the illustration on page 194.

If your toilet makes a hissing sound, the float valve may not

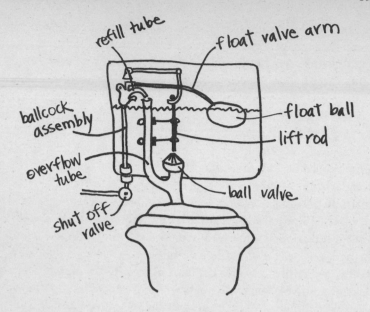

be closing all the way. Lift up on the arm and see if the hissing stops. If it does, bend the arm down an inch or more. This should cure it. Bend it carefully—if it's old, it may snap off. You can buy a new one, but if it snaps right where it screws into the ballcock assembly, that's something else again. You may be able to buy just the part that it screws into, or you may have to buy a new assembly. If the assembly sprays water all over the place even when you lift the float valve, or it's obviously damaged, get a new one.

Installing a New Ballcock

The worst part of a ballcock assembly job is the cramped space you work in. For a while you'll be on extremely intimate terms with your toilet bowl.

In one way or another, you've turned your water off. Flush the toilet and sponge the remaining water out of the tank. Then unscrew the float valve rod from the old assembly and set it aside. There are a couple of nuts under the tank that hold the assembly in place. Loosen the first one with your arc joint pliers or adjustable wrench, and let it slide down the water supply pipe. Then loosen the other one and lift out the assembly.

Take the old assembly to the hardware store. They will probably carry only one kind of replacement, and they'll tell you it will fit the toilet you have. It probably will, too. Install the new assembly by reversing the above procedure. Connect the little brass or plastic refill tube and run it over to and down inside the overflow tube. Sometimes the brass tubes won't reach your old overflow tube. Buy a small length of plastic tubing and use that instead. This tube helps keep tank water from being siphoned back into your water pipes. But don't let it hang down into the water inside the overflow tube, or it *will* siphon.

Replacing the Ball Valve

Maybe the ball valve doesn't seat right, in which case water keeps running out of the tank and into the toilet bowl. When you do a ball valve job, you can prop or tie the float valve up to cut off the water, you don't have to shut off the pipe that runs to the tank. Keep jiggling the toilet handle, lifting the ball valve and letting it drop until you see how the rods that hold it have to be adjusted. Bend the rods until the valve seats correctly.

A deteriorated valve is simple to replace: you just unscrew it and screw on a new one. There are replacement balls that are supposed to insure foolproof seating, but I haven't tried them so I don't know if they're all that great or not.

Whenever you're working inside a toilet, do it gently or you might break off the overflow tube. Then you'll have to replace that, too. It's not likely that everything inside an old toilet will need replacing, but if it does, it will cost about $15 if you do it yourself. If you have a plumber do it, it will probably run you $50 or more, so you might as well have him put in a whole new toilet.

Esoteric Fixtures and Their Replacement

On Lawrence Street we had to get a new toilet because the old one had been smashed. City water eats the insides out of toilets and water heaters (don't ask me what it's doing to *your* insides), so we got a toilet with plastic innards that the nasty stuff couldn't wreck. It was a medium priced "reverse trap" job, and the best known brand on the market. What could be wrong with that? We found out fast.

A few days after the toilet was installed, we had the gas company turn on our old water heater. When the man finished, Davene and her sister and I went shopping, warm with the knowledge that when we returned we'd at last have hot water in the house. We were gone for three hours. When we got back, Davene's sister went up to the bathroom and I went to the kitchen to get a drink of water.

I turned on the cold water tap and hot water came out. *Steaming* hot water. Oh no, I moaned, the plumber hooked the water heater into the cold water line. Grumbling, I turned on the hot water tap to get a glass of cold. This water was steaming too. That got me. How could both faucets run hot? Then from upstairs came a scream and the sound of the bathroom door flying open. "The toilet exploded!" my sister-in-law cried. I ran up the steps. She was lost in billows of steam. The toilet bubbled and spouted and roared, a minor Vesuvius. Then it dawned on me: the thermostat on the old water heater was broken and wouldn't shut off. So the whole time we were gone, the water had heated and heated and heated until it had backed into the cold water pipes. I opened all the faucets and turned the water heater off. We were lucky. Very lucky. The plumber had neglected to put a pressure relief valve in the hot water line. This valve is a safety device that opens before pressure in the line reaches a dangerously high level. When it opens, water pours out all over your cellar floor, but at least the water heater doesn't explode. If we had stayed out a little longer—blam!

When the clouds of steam thinned out, I looked inside the still-gurgling toilet tank. The plastic parts had buckled to surrealistic sculpture.

The plumber replaced them. But one thing he did not replace was a rubber gasket (around the overflow unit) which gave out two years later, undoubtedly because of undue stress during infancy. In any case, replacement would be easy—the most famous brand of toilet on the market, remember. I could not find a replacement for that gasket. I went to the company's largest Philadelphia distributor. They had never heard of a toilet like mine, was I sure it was an —— ——? What could I do, bring it in to prove it to them? Sorry, but they couldn't help me. Apparently the company had experimented with this toilet a couple of years before, then discarded the experiment—and I was stuck with it. I would've bought a whole new overflow unit, but standard replacement parts would not fit this baby.

I was not about to throw out a two-year-old toilet. I bought a tube of silicone rubber sealant and made myself a gasket. Luckily, it worked. I had learned a lesson: even if you buy a well-known brand, you have to watch yourself. Make sure you don't buy an experiment. Most toilet parts are interchangeable —but every once in a while you'll run into something non-standard that you want to avoid.

We have a Mansfield toilet in our present house. The Mansfield insides are different from most toilets, and I was careful to find out about the availability of replacement parts before I had it installed. It has plastic guts—great for city water—but of course that isn't why I bought it. I bought it because you can control the amount of water you use when you flush. You push down on the handle: if you let go, the Mansfield acts just like a regular toilet and uses all the water in the tank. But if you pull up on the handle, the water from the tank is immediately shut off. This saves a lot of water, and, if you have a pump, a lot of electricity as well.

You can save water with a regular toilet by bending the float valve arm down 2″ lower than its normal setting. This won't affect its flushing efficiency, and in the "average" family, this will save 20 gallons of water a day. Some people put a brick in the tank to displace water, but it's not nearly as effective a water-saver.

The Built-in Bathtub

Our old tub taught us another lesson. It was a high and handsome thing with brass fixtures. We painted the outside of it red and bathed happily for several years, though the drain stopper was broken and the finish was so worn you couldn't slip if you waxed your feet. Then we got the urge for a shower.

The tub sat away from the wall a few inches and it had rounded rims. We figured if we wanted a shower we'd have to box the tub in, or water would go everywhere. We talked it over with a carpenter and came up with a plan. He framed in the tub with 2 x 4s and plywood. Then we paneled the frame's sides with redwood strips that someone had thrown away, and the top of the frame—the part around the tub's rim—we tiled with tiny blue ceramic tiles. It was beautiful.

And impractical. When you box in a tub, you are almost always in for trouble. It is just about impossible to treat the area around the rim in any efficient way. Every time we showered, water would collect on the rim and pour onto the floor. We had to erect dikes of sponges to stem the tide. The situation was especially bad with guests: most of them could never get the sponges right, and they took much longer showers than we, who after a short while found ourselves sticking to a five minute limit.

Once when Arturo stayed with us he ecstatically announced after breakfast, "I am going to take a shower!" He had used our tub several times, I was confident he knew its hazards, and I didn't mention the sponges. After he'd been gone for ages, I went up and knocked, and found him mopping up a full inch of water over the entire floor (12 x 15 feet, remember) with every towel he could find. Grinning, he said, "I forgot the system."

So if you plan to build a shower around an old tub, be prepared.

Also consider whether or not you want to live with the dull and possibly rusted porcelain surface of an old tub. You can resurface old sinks and tubs with epoxy paint, but you can never hope to restore the finish to anything like the original. We never resurfaced a tub this way because we once lived with a tub painted (but not epoxied) with blue waves. The paint made it even duller, a Sargasso Sea, and it kind of turned us off to all tub painting.

We did do our shower walls on Lawrence Street with epoxy, however, and they held up well. We used a brush, and painted over both primed marine plywood and primed plaster. You can use this stuff right over old ceramic tiles, too. On fixtures, you'll get a better finish with a spray.

LEAKING FAUCETS

Your faucet chatters and shivers when you turn the water off. You forget about it and pretty soon it starts to drip. You need a new washer. Most diagrams of faucet insides scare you to death. I hope this one doesn't. The things are really not that complicated.

If the faucet dribbles water around the chrome nut, wrap adhesive tape around the nut to keep it from being scratched, and tighten it with your wrench. If that doesn't work, you'll have to operate. The water, remember, should be turned off.

You can usually do the job with just a screwdriver and a pair of arc joint pliers or a wrench. I find the pliers handier. Faucets vary widely in the details of their construction, and it would take

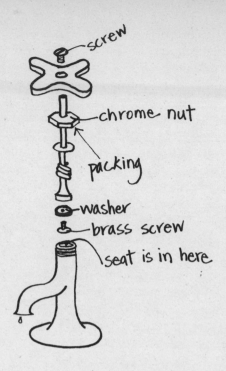

a little manual to talk about them all. Most of the old ones have a screw holding the handle on. Before you remove it, put the stopper in the sink so you don't lose the screw down the drain. Then take out the screw and remove the handle. This may not be so easy. Corrosion has probably stuck it to the spindle. Cover the handle with a rag, then tap it with a hammer and pry it up with an old screwdriver or other instrument. You may have to squirt some penetrating oil down there and wait 15 minutes or so. If you don't have penetrating oil, try iodine or peroxide.

Once the handle's off, the next step is to remove the chrome nut. Wrap adhesive tape around it, then turn counterclockwise with your pliers or wrench. Again, this may take some soaking in penetrating oil and some effort. Once you get the nut loose, you can unscrew the works of the faucet and see what gives. (You may now realize that you didn't have to unscrew the handle after all, that's how it is with some faucets. Oh well.)

Under the chrome nut there is probably a string-like packing wound around the stem of the faucet. If the faucet has been dribbling water around the nut, chances are this packing is chewed up and will have to be replaced. You just wrap a turn or two of new stuff around the stem. In a real pinch you can use cotton string, but there are graphite and teflon stem packings available at the hardware store that are much better.

Suppose you've had chattering or faucet drip. At the bottom of the stem is the washer. Or was the washer; it may be gone completely. You should also find a little brass screw that holds the washer in place, but it may have disappeared too. Most repair books assume the screw is still there and all you have to do is unscrew it and stick on a new washer. It is a dangerous assumption. I have opened up any number of faucets and found that the screw has succumbed to time and city water. It wouldn't be too bad if it dissolved completely, because you could take the stem to the hardware and get a new screw. But usually just the head of the screw crumbles off and the body remains in the screw hole, leaving it clogged. There is no way you are going to unclog it. How can you replace the washer?

I've used two methods. One is to cement a new washer in place with liquid epoxy. Take the stem to the hardware store and have them match the size of the washer for you. There are two shapes of washers, beveled and flat, and if there's nothing left of the old one it's going to be hard to tell which kind to use. You can get around this problem by using method number two: which is to make your own washer out of silicone sealer. Dry the end of the stem completely, then squeeze a ring of silicone in the spot where the old washer used to be. Let it harden for a day. I have done this several times, once for a very unusual shower control washer that I couldn't replace. This kind of washer, if given normal use, should hold up for several years.

Maybe you fix the washer and then after a month or two the

faucet starts leaking again. This probably means that the seat, the metal thing the washer presses into, is ragged and is tearing the washer to pieces.

Take the faucet apart again and check the condition of the washer. If it's chewed up, run your finger lightly and carefully inside the part of the faucet that's still attached to the sink. If it feels rough, see if you can take the old seat out. You'll need a good-size Allen (or "hex") wrench to remove it. Take it to the hardware store and get an exact replacement. New seats cost about a dime. If you can't get the seat out, you'll have to buy a seat-dressing tool (costs about $1.50). Get the hardware store to show you how it works. It can take the rough edges off the seat so it won't eat up your washers anymore.

LEAKS IN WATER PIPE

What if you have a small leak in a water pipe? You can buy a little rubber clamp to screw onto the pipe and stop the leak. What if the leak is in a spot you can't get a clamp on?

Once I stayed in a house with a small leak way up inside the shower wall. I didn't relish tearing out the back wall of the shower—which was lined with built-in shelves. So I turned off the water supply, dried the spot thoroughly by sticking a lamp up through the little access door between the shelves, then reached up through the door and smeared liquid epoxy around the joint with my finger. That was the end of the leak.

Back then, you had to wait hours for epoxy to harden. Now they have stuff that sets in five minutes. There are some glues that set almost instantly and hold incredibly, but they're dangerous. If I'd used one of them I'm sure they would've found me hours later, arm still sticking up inside the wall, hand cemented firmly to the pipe, and the shelves would've had to go after all.

11 YOUR ELECTRICITY

AS WITH PLUMBING, MOST CITIES WON'T LET YOU DO MUCH electrical work. In rural areas, however, you may be allowed to do a whole rewiring job, or at least everything but the installation of the "service entrance"—the circuit breaker panel and the heavy line that comes into the house. But if you're not going to tear the plaster off the walls of your old place, you don't want to rewire by yourself even if they'll let you. Why not? Because it's murder. Fishing wires through old walls is no job for an amateur. There are countless obstructions behind that old plaster, and will you ever give yourself a headache.

On Lawrence Street we signed a contract for a complete rewiring job at what seemed like a reasonable figure. The day the work began, I came home to find the electricians growling and cursing and attacking the third floor hallway walls with gigantic drills. They had made a distressing discovery: our partitions were not framed with studs, but with solid planks 3″ thick. These guys had to drill and chop for every electrical box they installed, and just about every wire they ran.

203

On Lambert Street we used the same electrician. (What a glutton for punishment!) On the third floor there, he ran into a double set of joists; one set ran from party wall to party wall as you'd expect, and another set ran on top of these in the opposite direction—as you'd never expect in your wildest dreams. I am sure that man is glad we moved to Maine.

DOING IT YOURSELF

If you've ripped out all the old plaster and lath and are left with nothing but studs, you might want to give the whole job a try. The hardest part is the planning: how many circuits to use, how to divide them, and where to put all the outlets and switches. This is almost a book in itself, and I can't go into it here. Sears puts out a helpful manual on electrical work and Richter's guide is good. Just remember to do everything the way the books tell you to—you don't want to fry. If you're careful, you can do an excellent job. As a matter of fact, one electrician told me that the amateur is usually more careful than the professional. He's so scared of making loose connections that he over-tightens them.

The actual installation of the system requires no special skills. It's well within the scope of the person who can do any sort of home repair at all. If you decide to do the job yourself, here are some tips to make things easier.

Cable

There are two major kinds of electrical cable, metal-sheathed ("BX") and non-metal-sheathed ("NM"). BX was all the rage for a while, but the newer plastic-covered cables have largely replaced it. The NM cable is much easier to work with and of course it can't rust like BX. I sure hope your local code approves it. Use the larger, #12 wire for circuits with outlets in them. It isn't that much harder to work with than #14, and it handles more current. You'll be plugging hi-fi sets, T.V.'s, maybe clothes irons, maybe even a floor sander into these outlets, and it's good to have the heavier wire. For circuits containing only lights, #14 is fine. Don't mix the two sizes of wire on any one circuit.

There is a difference in flexibility between the various brands of NM cable, and also a difference in the ease with which you can strip off the plastic outer covering. One brand of #12 cable may be quite rigid, and its outer covering may be so thick and tough that you can barely get your knife into it. It's good stuff, but leave it to the professionals. Other brands that meet the same basic standards are easy to bend and have a covering that, while perfectly safe and protective, is easy to strip off, too. By all means, try to get this kind. Sears makes wire like this. I guess because they expect that most of it will be used by amateurs.

You cut the plastic cable to the desired length with wire cutters. (I used an old pair of pruning shears, but you don't have to follow my example.) To cut the individual black, white, and ground wires, you can use the wire cutters or a pair of

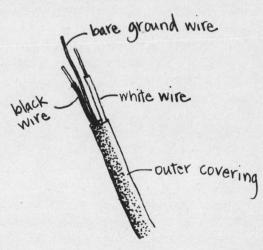

non-metallic electrical cable

electrician's pliers. If you are wiring the whole house, it will pay you to spend a couple of dollars for a wire stripper, a little device that instantly zips the covering off the tips of the black and white wires. If you're doing a small job, you can strip with your pocket knife.

When you slice the outer covering off the end of the cable, slice so your knife runs between either the black or white wire and the ground wire, and cut toward the bare ground wire. This way you won't accidentally cut through the covering on the black or white wires. Always remove enough of the outer covering to leave 8" of black, white, and ground wire exposed. It is easier to get this length of wire to fit inside an electrical box than it is to get a shorter length to fit.

Large Boxes

Use the large electrical boxes instead of the standard size. These are about $3\frac{1}{4}"$ high and $2\frac{1}{2}"$ deep instead of $3"$ high and $2"$ deep. This may not seem like a whole lot of difference, but it is. It's much easier to fit your outlets and switches into these boxes. If you're putting in a dimmer or a 3-way switch (larger than standard devices), or if you're using 3 wire (black, white, and red) cable, you'll really appreciate the bigger box.

Ground Wire

Electrical systems are "grounded." That is, they are connected to the earth by a wire that is attached to either the cold water line of the house or to a copper rod driven 8 feet below the earth's surface. This grounding serves two purposes: it protects the system from damage in case of accidental high voltage surges (from lightning, for example), and it protects you from getting a shock if there's a short circuit in the system.

Modern non-metallic cable electrical installations have a bare ground wire running through the entire system. In the circuit breaker panel or fuse box, this bare wire is attached to the same metal strip as the white wire, which is also a ground ("ground*ed* wire") but one that carries current; the bare wire ("ground*ing* wire") carries no current.

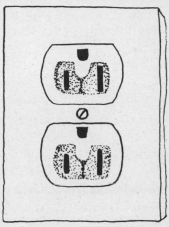

The bare ground wire is attached to each electrical outlet by a green screw that's part of the outlet. You loosen the screw, loop the wire around it, and tighten the screw again. The screw is at the *top* of the outlet. This means that the outlet is installed with the hole for the grounding pin up, like this: I know that looks weird, because you almost never see it done that way even though it's right. If you put the outlet in the usual way, grounding screw facing down, your head will be on the floor when you try to attach the wire to it. (3 prong cords are also designed to fit pin up into outlets. They're likely to fall out if the pin is down.)

Most electrical boxes are metal. In the event of a short, they could become "live," so they have to be grounded too—or you could get a shock just by touching a metal outlet plate. You ground the box by wrapping the cable's bare ground wire around a screw inserted in a hole in the box's back, then tightening the screw. The boxes don't come with the screws, you have to buy them separately. They are supposed to be green like those on outlets ("green grounding screws"), but you'll surely never find them in your hardware store. And if you ask the hardware people for them you'll be met with looks of scorn and derisive, perhaps off-color remarks. Ask for a box of   10 ½" or longer, "tapping" screws instead. These are the same thing, they just aren't green, and the hardware people will really think you know what you're talking about.

You can make your job easier if you buy a screwdriver with a screw-holding clip on its end; it's just about impossible to reach into the back of the box with your fingers.

Plastic Boxes

You can make the job *much* easier by using plastic boxes instead of metal, if your local code allows. Since plastic doesn't conduct electricity, you don't have to ground these boxes: they can never become "live." They come in the large size, are light and strong, are simply nailed onto studs or nailing strips, and require no clamps to hold the cable. (You just staple the cable to the stud within 8" of the box.) They are unbelievably sturdy once they're nailed in place. They are also cheaper than the metal boxes.

If you use plastic boxes, you don't attach the cable's ground wire to the box. You attach a piece of bare wire to the green screw on the outlet, run it over to the ground wires of the cable entering the box and the cable leaving the box, then screw all three wires together with a wire nut. (If the outlet is at the end of a run, there will be only one cable coming into the box, and only two wires to screw together.) At switches, you just screw the wires from the cables together.

Wire Nuts

I was used to the old twist-and-solder method of making electrical connections, and I thought you had to twist the wires together before you put the wire nuts on, but you don't. And the nuts work much better if you don't. Just keep the wires straight, hold them next to each other with their ends even, shove them all into the wire nut and turn it. The nut itself will twist the wires together tightly as you screw it on.

New Outlets

Install new outlets about 18″ above the floor. This way you won't have to bend so much when you plug and unplug, and you can reach outlets behind furniture more easily.

Also, if you're an amateur, you'd better install your outlets and switches (not just your boxes and cable) and check the whole system out before you put up your plasterboard. Then if anything is wrong, you can fix it without smashing up your walls.

SHOULD AN OLD HOUSE BE REWIRED?

Sometimes you'll read that you don't need to have an old house rewired, you can patch things up here and there and get by. You can, of course—I've seen lots of places that kept their old wiring and got along okay. And if you're in an old apartment, of course you'll live with the wires that exist. You'll replace broken switches and outlets, maybe extend the system on its surface and possibly eliminate any obviously frayed wires, but that's about it. You can do the same in an old house, too, but consider:

If the place was originally wired back in the twenties or thirties your service entrance will almost certainly be too small: 60 or even 30 amperes, and you should have at least 100. So you'll want to have this changed if nothing else. You will also have too few circuits and outlets. You'll be running extension cords all over the place, and you'll have to be careful about how many electrical devices you operate at one time, or you'll blow a lot of fuses. The wire will be all #14, which is okay for lighting circuits, but not for appliance circuits. In very old installations it will be "knob and tube"—separate black and white wires running through your floors in porcelain insulators and possibly running down the walls in wooden conduit. There's a chance that some of the insulation around this old wire has hardened and cracked, and you may have an unsafe condition. (It is remarkable, though, how often this kind of wiring is still in good condition: lifting a floorboard or two should let you know where you stand.) None of the system will be grounded, neither the outlets nor the electrical boxes, so there's a shock hazard. (You can live with this, we managed without seat belts for a long time, too.)

But the real danger in old wiring is the behind-the-scenes butchery that goes on from time to time. Our Lawrence Street house had not been touched in ages, and its electrical system, while inadequate, was safe. On Lambert Street it was a different story. Various owners had "modified" the system, and inside the walls we found splices simply twisted together loosely with no tape on them, eight cables wrapped together inside one junction box, no solder, no tape, no cover on the box, etc.

It's up to you. If you don't use many appliances and don't mind extension cords, you may find your old wiring satisfactory. If the house was wired in the forties or fifties, you very well may. If you have a 60 ampere entrance, you can usually have some special circuits run to handle an air conditioner or an electric dryer. But remember—you never know what's going on inside the walls. One of our old wires in Maine had 4" of its insulation chewed off by a rat. If you see signs of funny stuff, it's best to have the place done over.

Making Do

But suppose you decide to live with the old stuff, at least for a while. The repair you'll make most often is replacement of switches and outlets. This job is discussed in just about every home repair book ever published, so there's not much point in discussing it again. Remember to turn off the power to the circuit before you begin. In an old installation this means removing a fuse; in a new one, flipping a circuit breaker switch. In an apartment, it may mean throwing your neighbors into darkness and suspended time until you find the right thing to push or unscrew.

Old Outlets

On an old outlet, the black and white wires are looped around screws. (A switch has the black wire screwed to it at two points; the white wires are twisted together, and don't fool with them.) A newer type of outlet (and switch) does away with the need to loop the wires and screw them on, which was always a pain in the neck, and this is the kind of thing you want to buy.

All you do is strip some of the insulation off the black and white wires and shove them into holes in the back of the outlet or switch. There is a "strip gauge" on the device that shows you exactly how much bare wire should go into the hole. Scrape the wire with your pocket knife or some emery paper before you shove it in; this will assure a good contact. The hole for the white wire says "white" next to it, so you can't miss. Please don't, it's important that the wires go in the right places. (On a switch, of course, there will just be two holes for black wire.) The wires will lock in tightly, and you won't be able to pull them out unless you stick something in some other little holes to release them. Some of these devices have both screws and holes, so if you'd like to do it the old way, you have the option.

Your old system has no ground wire, so don't spend your money on grounded outlets. (If it has BX you may want to, though, as we'll see shortly.) And since your system doesn't have enough outlets, instead of buying the standard kind with just two pairs of slots, get the kind with four pairs of slots and you can avoid some extension cords.

Switches

Replace your switches with the mercury kind. They cost more, but they last far longer than the other ones they make nowadays. Be sure to install them "TOP" up so they work right.

If you're replacing a switch on a light that can be controlled at two places—in a hallway, for instance—you'll need a special kind of switch called a "3 way." So examine a switch carefully before you buy a new one. If there are three wires—two black and a red (or a black, a red, and a white) attached to it, you've got a 3 way. Don't take the wires off until you've got the replacement in your hand. You want to hook up the new switch in exactly the same way, and if you take out the old one before you go to the store, you'll probably forget how the wires went.

Frayed Insulation

Suppose when you pull out your old switch or outlet you find that the insulation at the ends of the wires is frayed. Unscrew the clamp that holds the cable, pull more cable into the box, cut back the wires to the point where the insulation is okay, tighten the clamp again, and install your new outlet.

You should be so lucky. There is probably no slack cable in the wall. And even if there is, if you have BX you'll probably have to punch a hole in your plaster to get it. The screws on the BX connector are on the outside of the electrical box, not on the inside, and you have to loosen them in order to pull more cable through.

If you have BX, hacksaw 8″ of the metal armor off, and the wires you'll expose will probably be good as new because they've had little contact with the air. This is a job. I'd just be content to cut the frayed ends off if there's still enough wire to make a connection.

If there's not enough wire? Well, I've seen a solution. You can bang a hole in the wall above your outlet, screw or nail a

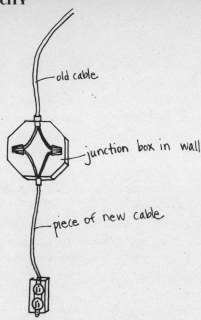

old cable

junction box in wall

piece of new cable

junction box inside the wall, and run a new piece of cable from this box to your outlet. (If the wire comes up through the floor, of course, you'll remove a floorboard instead.) Using wire nuts, attach the black and white wires of the old cable to the black and white wires of the new cable, then screw on the junction box cover.

Aside from smashing the wall and splitting your floorboard, there's another problem with this method: the National Electrical Code says that all junction boxes must be accessible. If anything goes wrong, you must be able to get at them without wrecking part of the house. If you put your floorboard back with screws, you're okay. Or if you install your junction box far enough forward so that its cover sticks out of the wall, that's okay too. So it's a good method to use in a closet or somewhere else where appearance isn't important. Of course, you *can* use it elsewhere. As electricians seem so fond of saying, "You can do anything in your own home."

Extending the Outlets

Let's say your wreck has a less than adequate service entrance and the TV picture shrinks when the washer goes on. There's only one window where the air conditioner can go, and the nearest outlet is across the room. Or there's no outlet where you want to make the toast. (Toasters draw about the same amount of power as air conditioners.) You just have to run an extension.

Wherever you can, you want to extend the electrical system with wire of the same capacity as that inside your walls. This will cut down on voltage drop. Doing this in several places may let you get by without having to have the house rewired right away.

You can, of course, extend the system by attaching new cable to an existing outlet. This means removing the outlet from the wall, running a new cable up inside the wall and into the outlet's electrical box, running the cable under the floor to the spot where you want the new outlet, running it up inside the wall at this point, chopping a hole in the wall, installing a new electrical box, and attaching the cable to the new outlet. This may not be too bad a deal if the job is on the first floor and there's a cellar below. You can drill up inside the wall from the cellar, run the cable across the cellar joists, drill another hole and pull the cable up through it and install your new box and outlet. But it's hard to know just where to drill your holes (you may come up in front of the wall in the room above instead of inside it). It isn't exactly easy to fish the wire up inside the wall either, God knows what you'll run into. And if you're living in an old apartment, you certainly don't want to mess with any of this. There must be an easier way.

There used to be. A few years ago you could buy a kit consisting of flexible #14 cable, a plug, an outlet, and little nails. You attached the cable to the outlet, screwed the outlet onto the baseboard, put the little nails through holes in the cable and tacked the cable to the baseboard, attached the plug, stuck it into an existing outlet, and you were set.

This stuff has disappeared. I don't know what happened to it, I guess it was too easy to install. If you find some, you're in luck. The cord is flat and unobtrusive and if you paint it you'll hardly notice it. Sears has a rather elaborate plastic version of this sort of thing, but it's bulky-looking and expensive.

The cheapest way out is to make your own heavy-duty extension out of indoor-outdoor electrical cable, the kind approved for surface installations in workshops, etc. Buy #14 wire. You'll need a length of the cable, a surface-mounted outlet, and a plug. The best plug is the kind that lets the cord lie flat against the wall and parallel with the baseboard. This is the kind Sears sells with its plastic set, and you can buy it separately. Attach the plug to one end of the wire, the outlet to the other, and secure the wire to the baseboard with electrical staples or plastic nail-on cable straps (Sears sells them, too). This will get the job done, but it doesn't look that great.

For more money, you can make the line out of the kind of extension cord you use for power tools. These are flat, highly flexible cables, usually with yellow or orange jackets. (Don't buy the round kind.) They come in lengths of 25 feet and up. They usually contain #16 wire, which is okay, but get #14 wire if you can. These extensions have a grounding wire in them, so they have 3 slot outlets and 3 prong plugs. You can use the plug that comes with them, but if your existing outlet is in your baseboard, it's better to snip the attached plug off and use the other kind so your wire can parallel the baseboard without kinking.

If you use the plug that comes with the cord, you will have to remove the grounding pin or the plug won't fit into the 2 slot outlets you have in your wall. If you have BX cable in your wall, you have another option: you can replace your present 2 slot outlet with a 3 slot outlet. All your boxes are grounded by the BX cable's metal armor. You can take a piece of bare copper wire (if you don't have any around, visit a construction site and pick up a piece of scrap), attach it to the back of the outlet box with a tapping screw, attach the other end to the green screw on the outlet, and you've got yourself a grounded outlet. This is important when you're hooking up a washer or an air conditioner: it can save you a mean jolt. If you don't have BX cable in your walls (or cable with ground wire, which is highly unlikely in an old system) you can't ground your outlet, so break off the grounding pin with your pliers.

You can't use the outlet that comes with the extension, because there's no way to attach it firmly to the baseboard, so cut the cord to the proper length and attach a surface outlet. Screw the outlet to the baseboard and secure the cord to the baseboard with little nails. The cord has two deep grooves in it. The ground wire runs between these grooves and the black and white wires run on either side of them. You can split the thin plastic in either of these grooves with an ice pick, and stick the little nails through the holes. Don't nail through any wires. If you're careful, you'll be okay. Stick the plug into your existing outlet. You'll have a flat, neat extension that will blend with the baseboard when painted.

If you're hooking up an air conditioner or washer and you haven't been able to ground the outlet, you should ground the appliance itself. Screw a length of copper wire to the frame of the appliance and clamp it to a radiator or cold water pipe. The hardware store sells clamps for this purpose.

Circuit Savers

One final tip to make life with an old wiring system easier. Replace your old fuses with "circuit savers." These are fuses with buttons in them that you reset just like the switches on a circuit breaker panel. They never "blow," they just "trip," and you don't ever have to buy new ones.

Postscript

Not long ago I pulled a muscle in my back two-thirds of the way through a doorway framing job. It was the front doorway that I was working on, and after one night of wildly flapping plastic sheeting and no improvement in the muscle, I conceded defeat and called in a carpenter to finish the job. (I was lucky enough to steal one away from work on a neighbor's house.)

The guy set the door in the opening and asked, "Who framed the rest of this?"

I reluctantly confessed I was the culprit.

"Not bad," the guy said. "Half the birds I work with couldn't do that good."

My back stopped hurting, my spirits soared, I went into the old "aw shucks" routine. "I was lucky," I said. "I'm just an amateur. I still have an awful lot to learn."

The carpenter smiled. "I've been doing this work all my life," he said, "and let me tell you a secret. Every morning when I get up for work I have this fear that this will be the day—the day I run into something I just can't handle."

217

Helpful Publications

Burbank, Nelson. *House Construction Details*, 6th ed. New York: Simmons-Boardman Co., 1968.

Cobb, Hubbard. *How to Buy and Remodel the Older House*. New York: Macmillan Co., 1970.

Day, Richard. *The Practical Handbook of Plumbing and Heating*. New York: Fawcett Publications, 1969.

NAHB Research Foundation. *Insulation Manual*. P. O. Box 1627, Rockville, Maryland: NAHB Research Foundation, 1971.

Richter, H. P. *Wiring Simplified*. Minneapolis, Minnesota: Park Publishing Co., 1971.

Staff of *The Family Handyman* Magazine. *America's Handyman Book*. New York: Charles Scribner's Sons, 1970.

United States Department of Agriculture. *Wood-Frame House Construction*. Washington, D.C.: Government Printing Office, 1970.

Wagner, Willis. *Modern Carpentry*. S. Holland, Illinois: The Goodheart-Willcox Co., 1969.

Tools and Materials

Brookstone Company, 16 Brookstone Building, Peterborough, New Hampshire 03458. This company sells unusual tools. Examples: a super electric paint remover and a diamond-tipped glass cutter. Catalog: twenty-five cents.

Epoxy in bulk can be purchased from: Allied Resin Corporation, East Weymouth, Massachusetts 02189; Chem Tech, 4481 Greenwold Road, Cleveland, Ohio 44121; Miller-Stephenson Chemical Company, Box 623, Danbury, Connecticut 06810.

Fluidmaster, 1800 Via Burton, Anaheim, California 92805. The Fluidmaster model 200 ballcock is described as "non-corrosive, extremely quiet"; it works with the water pressure instead of against it like standard ballcocks. It looks terrific. I haven't tried it, but it's something you should know about. They say it fits all toilets.

Quaker City Manufacturing Company, 701 Chester Pike, Sharon Hill, Pennsylvania 19079. They make "Quaker Window Channels," sash balances for old sash.

Rollers by Baker, Brandon, Vermont 05733. Makes paint rollers with soft bodies that conform to rough surfaces and have a built-in brush.

A Home Repair Glossary

allen wrench

Allen Wrench: An L-shaped hexagonal wrench that fits into recessed-head screws. Also called hex wrench.

Arc Joint Pliers: Pliers with very long handles that provide great leverage.

Baseboard: The board that runs along the bottom edge of a wall and contacts the floor, concealing the joint between the floor and wall.

Batt: A rectangular piece of insulation, usually about 2 feet wide and 4 feet long.

Beam: A piece of lumber that supports a load. Joists and rafters are beams.

Bearing Wall: A wall that helps to hold up part of a house or other structure. (Also called "load-bearing wall".)

Blanket: A long roll of insulation.

Bleeding: Staining of fresh paint by sap, old paint, blood, crayon, etc.

Box Nail: Similar to a common nail, but with a thinner shank (the part that penetrates the wood).

BX Cable: Electrical cable with a flexible steel outer covering. Also called armored cable.

Casement Window: A window with sash hinged along the side of the window frame. The sash open in or out instead of up and down.

Casing: The trim around the front of a doorjamb or window frame.

Caulk: A flexible, waterproof compound used to seal exterior cracks and keep out water, air, and cold.

Cement: A mixture of Portland cement, sand and water. See "Portland cement."

Cold Chisel: An all-steel chisel used primarily on masonry.

Common Nail: The standard nail used most frequently in construction.

Concrete: A mixture of Portland cement, sand, gravel and water. Concrete is very strong and is used for foundations, floors, posts, and sidewalks.

Crawl Space: A shallow area under the first floor of a basementless house. Or: A shallow space between the top floor of a house and the roof.

Cripples: The short pieces of stud above a header. See "header."

Dimension Lumber: Lumber 2″ to 5″ thick, up to 12″ wide, and any length. Joists, studs, rafters are dimension lumber.

Double Hung Window: A window with an upper and a lower sash that slide up and down.

Finishing Nail: A nail with a relatively thin shank and a small head that can be easily sunk below the surface of a board with a nail set.

Flashing: Material used above door and window frames, around chimneys and over joints in walls and roofs to keep out water. Flashing is usually aluminum, sometimes copper, lead, or other material.

Furring: Strips of wood or metal applied to a wall or ceiling that provide an even base for a covering material such as plasterboard, ceiling tile, or paneling.

Galvanized Nails: Nails with a zinc coating that inhibits rust. Used out-of-doors and for extra holding power. Common, box, and finishing nails are all available galvanized.

Glazier's Points: Small pieces of metal used to hold panes of glass in place while glazing compound is applied. See "push points."

Glazing Compound: A putty-like material used to hold a pane of glass in a sash and to waterproof the joints between sash and glass.

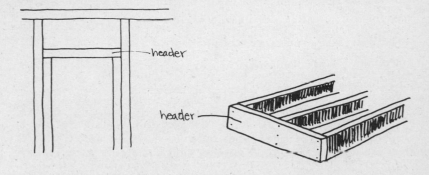

Header: A beam fastened at right angles across the ends of other beams. Or: A horizontal load-bearing member over a doorway or opening. (Also called a lintel.)

Insulation Board: Usually made of wood fibers and usually ½" thick, 4 feet wide and 8 feet long. Rigid board is used as outside sheathing, and a softer, more flexible board ("celotex") is used inside buildings as a wall and ceiling finish. Although it's called "insulation board," a single layer of this material actually provides little resistance to heat flow.

Insulation, thermal: Material that slows the rate at which heat flows out of a structure.

Jamb: The lining around the top and sides of a doorway or window.

Joists: The parallel beams that provide support for flooring and ceiling materials. Usually made of 2 x 8, 2 x 10, or 2 x 12 dimension lumber.

Junction Box: A box in which electrical wires are joined together. Can be either metal or plastic, square or octagonal.

Lath: Material nailed to studs or joists to provide a base for plaster. Lath may be strips of wood, metal mesh, or gypsum board.

Masonry: Brick, stone, concrete or cement block held together with mortar.

Mortar: A mixture of Portland cement, sand, hydrated lime and water used to hold brick, stone, etc., together or to cover a masonry surface (stucco).

Mortise: A hole, slot, or depression into which something fits or passes. Hinges and locks often fit into mortises.

Mullions: The dividers that hold panes of glass in a window sash.

Nail Set: A cylindrical, pointed piece of steel that is struck with a hammer and used to sink nails below the surface of the material that they have been driven into. It looks a lot like a short, metal pencil.

NM Cable: Electrical cable with an outer covering of plastic or fabric.

Oakum: A hemp fiber rope used to fill deep cracks.

On Center: The spacing of studs, rafters, joists, etc. from the center of one member to the center of the next. Studs are usually spaced either 16″ or 24″ on center.

Particle Board: Wood flakes and chips bonded together with water-proof glue to form a rigid board. Particle board comes in 4 x 8 foot sheets like plywood and is usually ⅜″ or ⅝″ thick. Less expensive than plywood.

Partition: A wall that divides space within a structure.

Party Walls: The shared, load-bearing side walls of structures that are joined together, such as row houses and twin houses.

Penetrating Oil: A solvent that dissolves rust.

Penny (or "d"): A term used to denote nail length. The higher the number, the longer the nail. An 8d nail is 2½″ long, a 10d nail is 3″ long.

Perlite: A base coat plaster made of volcanic rock.

Plasterboard: Sheets of gypsum plaster covered on both sides by heavy paper. Used to cover studs on the inside of a house. Also called drywall, Sheetrock, and wallboard.

Plate: A horizontal piece of lumber into which vertical members are fastened. A stud partition has a sole plate and a top plate.

Plumb: Straight up and down; exactly vertical.

Portland Cement: A gray, fine powder made of clay, chalk, limestone, and other materials. The bonding material in cement, mortar, and concrete.

Primer: The first coat of paint applied to a surface that has been prepared for painting. Also: A paint especially formulated to seal and fill a surface and provide a base for finish paints.

Push Points: A newer type of glazier's point that can be easily pushed into the sash with a screwdriver.

Rafters: The parallel beams that support roof loads.

Ringed Nail: A nail with evenly spaced grooves along its shank. The grooving greatly increases the nail's holding power.

Sash: The parts of a window that contain the glass.

Sash Balances: Metal channels in which the sash of double hung windows slide up and down.

Sheathing: The covering applied to the outside of a building, directly over the rafters and studs. Usually boards, plywood, or rigid insulation board.

Shim: A thin piece of material, usually wood, used to fill a gap or depression.

Sills: Large beams on which the floor joists or walls of a structure rest. Also: The horizontal, lower members of an opening; for example, windowsills.

Soil Stack: The main waste line in a plumbing system.

Studs: The vertical framing members of walls. Usually 2 x 3 or 2 x 4 dimension lumber.

Subfloor: The material applied directly on top of floor joists, over which the finish floorboards are laid.

Toenailing: Driving a nail at an angle through one piece of wood and into another.

toenailing

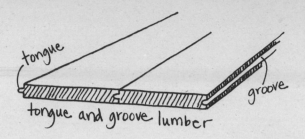

tongue

tongue and groove lumber

groove

Tongue-and-Groove Lumber: Boards with channels and protruding beads that fit into each other. Also called matched lumber.

Underlayment Nails: Ringed nails designed for fastening underlayments such as plywood and particle board into old floors or into joists.

Vapor Barrier: A material applied over insulation to cut down on the flow of water vapor through walls, ceilings, and floors.

INDEX